**New Directions for
Teaching and Learning**

Catherine M. Wehlburg
EDITOR-IN-CHIEF

Doing the Scholarship of Teaching and Learning: Measuring Systematic Changes to Teaching and Improvements in Learning

Regan A. R. Gurung
Janie H. Wilson

EDITORS

Number 136 • Winter 2013
Jossey-Bass
San Francisco

DOING THE SCHOLARSHIP OF TEACHING AND LEARNING: MEASURING SYSTEMATIC CHANGES TO TEACHING AND IMPROVEMENTS IN LEARNING
Regan A. R. Gurung, Janie H. Wilson (eds.)
New Directions for Teaching and Learning, no. 136
Catherine M. Wehlburg, Editor-in-Chief

Microfilm copies of issues and articles are available in 16 mm and 35 mm, as well as microfiche in 105 mm, through University Microfilms, Inc., 300 North Zeeb Road, Ann Arbor, MI 48106-1346.

NEW DIRECTIONS FOR TEACHING AND LEARNING (ISSN 0271-0633, electronic ISSN 1536-0768) is part of The Jossey-Bass Higher and Adult Education Series and is published quarterly by Wiley Subscription Services, Inc., A Wiley Company, at Jossey-Bass, One Montgomery Street, Suite 1200, San Francisco, CA 94104-4594. POSTMASTER: Send address changes to New Directions for Teaching and Learning, Jossey-Bass, One Montgomery Street, Suite 1200, San Francisco, CA 94104-4594.

New Directions for Teaching and Learning is indexed in CIJE: Current Index to Journals in Education (ERIC), Contents Pages in Education (T&F), Educational Research Abstracts Online (T&F), ERIC Database (Education Resources Information Center), Higher Education Abstracts (Claremont Graduate University), and SCOPUS (Elsevier).

INDIVIDUAL SUBSCRIPTION RATE (in USD): $89 per year US/Can/Mex, $113 rest of world; institutional subscription rate: $311 US, $351 Can/Mex, $385 rest of world. Single copy rate: $29. Electronic only–all regions: $89 individual, $311 institutional; Print & Electronic–US: $98 individual, $357 institutional; Print & Electronic–Can/Mex: $98 individual, $397 institutional; Print & Electronic–rest of world: $122 individual, $431 institutional.

EDITORIAL CORRESPONDENCE should be sent to the editor-in-chief, Catherine M. Wehlburg, c.wehlburg@tcu.edu.

www.josseybass.com

Contents

FROM THE SERIES EDITOR

About This Publication

Since 1980, *New Directions for Teaching and Learning* (NDTL) has brought a unique blend of theory, research, and practice to leaders in postsecondary education. NDTL sourcebooks strive not only for solid substance but also for timeliness, compactness, and accessibility.

The series has four goals: to inform readers about current and future directions in teaching and learning in postsecondary education, to illuminate the context that shapes these new directions, to illustrate these new direction through examples from real settings, and to propose ways in which these new directions can be incorporated into still other settings.

This publication reflects the view that teaching deserves respect as a high form of scholarship. We believe that significant scholarship is conducted not only by researchers who report results of empirical investigations but also by practitioners who share disciplinary reflections about teaching. Contributors to NDTL approach questions of teaching and learning as seriously as they approach substantive questions in their own disciplines, and they deal not only with pedagogical issues but also with the intellectual and social context in which these issues arise. Authors deal on the one hand with theory and research and on the other with practice, and they translate from research and theory to practice and back again.

About This Volume

The Scholarship of Teaching and Learning (SoTL) is a crucial part of how higher education understands and shares its pedagogy. In theory, SoTL is a part of every faculty member, administrator, and (at least indirectly) student as they participate within their disciplinary courses and majors. SoTL can be a powerful force by bringing new ideas, practices, and findings into the academy and many faculty are involved in this process of scholarship. The authors within this volume point out that SoTL is linked to pedagogy, assessing learning, and faculty development. These chapters provide an empirically based guide to conducting SoTL research, clarify the uses of SoTL, and provide support for those faculty involved in this worthy endeavor. Faculty, department chairs, and administrators will find this volume to be exceedingly useful as a sort of manual on SoTL and will use this information for years to come.

Catherine Wehlburg
Editor-in-Chief

1

This chapter provides a brief history of the Scholarship of Teaching and Learning (SoTL), delineates the main audience for this volume, and presents a framework of the volume with a preview of each chapter.

Advancing Scholarly Research on Teaching and Learning

Regan A. R. Gurung, Janie H. Wilson

The Scholarship of Teaching and Learning (SoTL) is getting popular. There is a brand new journal for it coming out almost every year. *Teaching and Learning Inquiry* launched in 2013, and *SoTL in Psychology* starts accepting submissions in 2014 to launch in 2015, joining a host of other journals publishing research on teaching and learning (e.g., *Teaching of Psychology* and *International Journal for the Scholarship of Teaching and Learning*). In *The Scholarship of Teaching and Learning Reconsidered,* Pat Hutchings, Mary Taylor Huber, and Anthony Ciccone (2011) of the Carnegie Foundation for the Advancement of Teaching recently showcased how SoTL has been integrated into higher education and impacts teaching and learning.

SoTL should be an integral part of every academic's life, not only representing the pinnacle of effortful teaching but also standing side by side with more conventional disciplinary scholarship. In fact, SoTL "brings powerful new principles and practices" into the debate about key academic questions such as what students need to know and should be able to do (Hutchings, Huber, and Ciccone 2011, 3). As a result of faculty buy-in and an interest in best teaching practices, more scholars are providing tips on how to be a good teacher (e.g., Buskist and Benassi 2012) and how to use empirical evidence to guide pedagogy choices (Schwartz and Gurung 2012). Simultaneously, higher education institutions around the country have increased their focus on assessment, and a number of books provide helpful guides to assessment in the classroom (e.g., Dunn et al. 2011; Suskie 2009). In an almost parallel development, advocates of SoTL note that SoTL is linked to all three areas: conducting SoTL is the hallmark of a good teacher, SoTL helps a teacher pick pedagogy, and SoTL provides the framework for classroom assessment. SoTL is now seen to be critical to assessing learning as well as faculty development (Hutchings, Huber, and Ciccone 2011). Although guides

New Directions for Teaching and Learning, no. 136, Winter 2013 © 2013 Wiley Periodicals, Inc.
Published online in Wiley Online Library (wileyonlinelibrary.com) • DOI: 10.1002/tl.20071

to conducting SoTL are available (e.g., Bishop-Clark and Dietz-Uhler 2012; McKinney 2007; Savory, Burnett, and Goodburn 2007), none of the existing books go beyond basic approaches to classroom research. We conceptualized this volume to build on the existing literature and provide pedagogical researchers with helpful tips in key areas of the scholarly process.

A Little Background

Boyer (1990) popularized the term "scholarship of teaching," although caring teachers have practiced the kind of work to which this term refers for many years. In more than 20 years following Boyer's work, the term SoTL has been dissected, defined, redefined, and modified (see Smith 2012, for a more detailed history of the evolution of the term). SoTL entails intentional, systematic reflections on teaching and learning resulting in peer-reviewed products made public (Potter and Kustra 2011). This volume brings together experienced practitioners of SoTL and builds on the skills and experiences teachers already have, providing thorough guidelines to help faculty implement and measure systematic changes to teaching and document potential improvements in student learning. Chapters follow the main stages of the research process (e.g., designing a study, measuring outcomes, and analyzing data) and provide exemplars of best practices taken from the published literature. Conceptualized as a catalyst and guide for workshops on SoTL and written for the teacher who wants to formally investigate learning, this volume had its roots in the Society for the Teaching of Psychology's first SoTL research/writing workshop in 2011. Although workshop participants had some experience with SoTL and were passionate teachers, it was clear that no existing resource answered the majority of questions that arose. This exact sentiment was expressed by many attendees at the 2011 International Society for the Scholarship of Teaching and Learning (ISSOTL) Conference. This volume is designed to fill the void and provide a helpful resource for anyone interested in documenting, learning, and systematically improving their teaching.

We provide an up-to-date, empirically based guide to conducting the Scholarship of Teaching and Learning. Authors elucidate the nuances of conducting SoTL, distinguish this form of research from other forms of scholarship, clarify the utility of SoTL to faculty as well as departments and Universities, and provide a useful aid to many faculty who may have heard of SoTL but have not joined the wave of change. Unlike existing publications, this work includes explicit examples of SoTL, demonstrating a variety of research designs, offering several forms of statistical analyses, and providing exemplars for both novices and experts alike.

Who Is This Volume For?

Those who would find this volume of interest fall into three categories: centers of teaching and learning/faculty development centers, administration such as department chairs, and individual faculty/teachers and researchers in the field of SoTL. Located at most institutions of higher learning, centers of teaching and learning are available to faculty as a resource to continually improve teaching. This volume is the type of resource that could assist center directors when creating teaching workshops and as a resource when working with individual faculty members or graduate students. Finally, we anticipate that this volume would serve as a starting point for those who are new to the classroom and are making decisions regarding useful pedagogy.

Given that documenting teaching using SoTL is also a major improvement over the exclusive use of student evaluations, more departments favor faculty formalizing their assessments using SoTL (Bernstein et al. 2009; Hutchings, Huber, and Ciccone 2011). This volume will likely be a good resource for department chairs who want to foster SoTL but who do not have the resources and the training to do so. In fact, administrators at higher levels may find the volume useful if scholarship in teaching is valued at their institution.

This volume would also be a valuable resource for individual faculty at all levels of education, with particular appeal to community college teachers, four-year college and university professors, and graduate student assistants who teach. It would also be very appropriate for graduate courses on teaching and learning in higher education and can be especially useful reading for new and midlevel faculty. Importantly, this volume would be appropriate to a wide audience given not only its applicability to teachers at different stages of their careers but also due to its cross-discipline appeal. We anticipate that this volume will be a manual for the prospective SoTL scholar. We are grateful to the authors who provide their expertise in this volume and generously help others enjoy the teacher-scholar role.

An Overview of This Volume

Additional guides introduce SoTL (Gurung and Schwartz 2012; McKinney 2007; Savory, Burnett, and Goodburn 2007); however, most of these books provide readers with the basics. This volume not only is accessible to the novice SoTL researcher but also provides readers with challenges that will motivate them to engage in the suggested activities. We include many key features aimed to help both teachers new to research and SoTL and also researchers who may have a long list of scholarly publications in nonpedagogical areas.

Each chapter answers key questions that starting SoTL researchers raise. In Chapter 2, Dickson and Treml bridge the gap between assessment and SoTL. Many instructors who see the value of assessment do not necessarily see assessment as a form of SoTL and often do not publish the fruits of their assessment labors. Conversely, and perhaps somewhat strangely, many SoTL practitioners do not recognize the extent to which their pedagogical research is assessment (Gurung and Landrum 2012). In many ways, Dickson and Treml help set the stage to increase SoTL in this age of assessment-minded expectations in higher education.

In Chapters 3 and 4, Bartsch addresses two major aspects of SoTL research: validity (Chapter 3) and practicality (Chapter 4). SoTL research cannot be conducted in the same way as social-science or natural-science research. The classroom is not a laboratory. By the same token, SoTL needs to live up to standards. Recent publications provide benchmarks for SoTL in psychology (Wilson-Doenges and Gurung 2013) and a universal set of good practices for SoTL (Felten 2013), but trying to satisfy good practices is challenging. Bartsch's chapters help pedagogical researchers navigate this tricky ground, providing different designs for research, ways to counter threats to validity, and methods to conduct practical research ethically.

In Chapter 5, Wilson-Doenges tackles data from approved SoTL research. Of course data require statistical analysis in some form, and the author of this chapter offers many options. Are statistics important to SoTL when faculty from many disciplines are not trained to conduct analyses? Certainly, some SoTL faculty from the humanities and the arts feel pressured to know how to design experiments and conduct statistical analyses (Grauerholz and Main 2013). Wilson-Doenges makes the case for the use of statistics in SoTL and provides some key strategies and techniques. Her approach makes statistics accessible to teacher-scholars across disciplines.

After designing a valid and practical study, the methodology must be reviewed by peers. In Chapter 6, Martin addresses a key area of the SoTL research process: getting approval to conduct SoTL. Every SoTL study should have Institutional Review Board (IRB) approval. What are the different types of IRB approval? When do you need each type of approval, and when is traditional informed consent appropriate? Martin unpacks the mystique of the IRB process, including when written consent is needed and more importantly, when it is not needed. Even seasoned researchers may discover hitherto unknown nuances of the process in this engaging exposé of the process.

After study approval, data collection, and data analysis, SoTL researchers must write a manuscript and seek publication. Chapters 7 and 8 focus on these two different processes. Smith (Chapter 7) provides tips on how to write strong academic papers, and Christopher (Chapter 8) provides suggestions on how to increase the likelihood of getting published. Both chapters provide useful and practical guidelines to get your research project from ideas and data to a manuscript ready for review. Chapter authors have served as editors of a SoTL journal and bring their years of experience to bear on the topic of writing.

Finally, in Chapter 9, Schwartz and Haynie address how SoTL can serve as a tool for faculty development with a focus on the role of teaching-and-learning centers on campus. SoTL is difficult to conduct in isolation, and institutional support is crucial. How can a campus or university center help faculty accomplish SoTL? What are key programs that learning centers should provide? The authors answer these questions and many more.

SoTL is now enjoying increased visibility and is relevant to academic life in a number of ways. Not only is there growing evidence that SoTL benefits faculty members as they engage in meaningful scholarship, this type of scholarship is also associated with student learning. We hope the present volume catalyzes more SoTL as we move toward an ever-growing understanding of teaching and learning in academic settings.

References

Bernstein, D., W. Addison, C. Altman, D. Hollister, K. Meera, L. R. Prieto, C. A. Rocheleau, and C. Shore. 2009. "Toward a Scientist-Educator Model of Teaching Psychology." In *The NCUEP: A Blueprint for the Future*, edited by D. Halpern, 29–46. Washington, DC: American Psychological Association.

Bishop-Clark, C., and B. Dietz-Uhler. 2012. *Engaging in the Scholarship of Teaching and Learning: A Guide to the Process and How to Develop a Project from Start to Finish*. Sterling, VA: Stylus.

Boyer, E. L. 1990. *Scholarship Reconsidered: Priorities of the Professoriate*. San Francisco: Jossey-Bass.

Buskist, W., and V. A. Benassi, eds. 2012. *Effective College and University Teaching: Strategies and Tactics for the New Professoriate*. Los Angeles: Sage.

Dunn, D. S., M. A. McCarthy, S. C. Baker, and J. S. Halonen. 2011. *Using Quality Benchmarks for Assessing and Developing Undergraduate Programs*. San Francisco: Jossey-Bass.

Felten, P. 2013. "Principles of Good Practice in SoTL." *Teaching and Learning Inquiry* 1: 121–126.

Grauerholz, L., and E. Main. 2013. "Fallacies of SoTL: Rethinking How We Conduct Our Research." In *The Scholarship of Teaching and Learning in and across the Disciplines*, edited by K. McKinney, 152–168. Bloomington: Indiana University Press.

Gurung, R. A. R., and R. E. Landrum. 2012. "Assessment and the Scholarship of Teaching and Learning." In *Assessing Teaching and Learning in Psychology: Current and Future Perspectives*, edited by D. Dunn, S. C. Baker, C. M. Mehrotra, R. E. Landrum, and M. McCarthy, 159–171. Belmont, CA: Wadsworth Cengage Learning.

Gurung, R. A. R., and B. M. Schwartz. 2012. *Optimizing Teaching and Learning: Practicing Pedagogical Research*. Malden, MA: Wiley-Blackwell.

Hutchings, P., M. T. Huber., and A. Ciccone. 2011. *The Scholarship of Teaching and Learning Reconsidered: Institutional Impact*. San Francisco: Jossey-Bass.

McKinney, K. 2007. *Enhancing Learning through the Scholarship of Teaching and Learning*. Bolton, MA: Anker.

Potter, M. K., and E. Kustra. 2011. "The Relationship between Scholarly Teaching and SoTL: Models, Distinctions, and Clarifications." *International Journal for the Scholarship of Teaching and Learning*, 5. Retrieved from http://digitalcommons.georgiasouthern.edu/int_jtl/80/.

Savory, P., A. N. Burnett, and A. Goodburn. 2007. *Inquiry into the College Classroom: A Journey towards Scholarly Teaching*. Bolton, MA: Anker.

Schwartz, B. M., and R. A. R. Gurung. 2012. *Evidence-Based Teaching in Higher Education.* Washington, DC: American Psychological Association.

Smith, R. A. 2012. "Benefits of Using SoTL in Picking and Choosing Pedagogy." In *Evidence-Based Teaching for Higher Education,* edited by B. M. Schwartz and R. A. R. Gurung, 7–22. Washington, DC: American Psychological Association.

Suskie, L. 2009. *Assessing Student Learning: A Common Sense Guide,* 2nd ed. San Francisco: Jossey-Bass/Wiley.

Wilson-Doenges, G., and R. A. R. Gurung. 2013. "Benchmarks for Scholarly Investigations of Teaching and Learning." *Australian Journal of Psychology,* 65 (1): 63–70. doi:10.1111/ajpy.12011.

REGAN A. R. GURUNG *is associated with the University of Wisconsin–Green Bay.*

JANIE H. WILSON *is associated with Georgia Southern University.*

2

Coordinating SoTL and assessment efforts strengthens the processes of inquiry, evidence, and innovation that lead to the continual improvement of student learning. Examples are provided for how to work collaboratively with colleagues to use these processes to continually inform the teaching practices within classrooms, academic programs, and institutions.

Using Assessment and SoTL to Enhance Student Learning

K. Laurie Dickson, Melinda M. Treml

To begin, we ask you to think for a moment about the questions that drive SoTL: Are my students learning? How do I know that they are learning? Is my teaching helping students learn? What opportunities can I design that best facilitate students' learning? SoTL typically involves an instructor asking questions about the impact of his/her teaching on students' learning in an individual course.

Now, ask those same questions of your academic program or institution: Are students learning what we, as faculty, want them to learn by the time they graduate with a degree in our discipline? How do we know what they learned? Is the design of our curriculum facilitating our students' learning? What opportunities can we intentionally design to best facilitate students' learning consistently from the first to the last class in our program? With these questions, you have entered the realm of program-level assessment. Assessment typically involves a group of faculty asking questions about the impact of their collective teaching on students' learning in the academic program.

As you can see, assessment and SoTL are driven by similar questions and share common foundations (Hutchings, Huber, and Ciccone 2011). They both:

- focus on student learning;
- use systematic, evidence-based approaches to examine student learning;
- document what and how well students are learning; and
- use empirical evidence to drive the enhancement of student learning.

New Directions for Teaching and Learning, no. 136, Winter 2013 © 2013 Wiley Periodicals, Inc.
Published online in Wiley Online Library (wileyonlinelibrary.com) • DOI: 10.1002/tl.20072

A key, yet complementary, difference is that rather than individual faculty focusing on individual classes, program-level assessment has an eye toward how classes meet the program's learning goals and how faculty as a group help students achieve learning outcomes.

As teaching scholars, we must objectively examine the effectiveness of our educational practices in our courses and programs rather than relying on our perceptions or anecdotes. Both faculty and departments need evidence that students are learning and that we are facilitating that learning through our pedagogy and curriculum. Thus, approaches to assessment at both levels must build on a foundation of empirical results.

This chapter will highlight how SoTL and assessment can interface. Building bridges between SoTL and assessment can provide faculty with an integrated web of evidence that can and should be used to improve student learning (Hutchings, Huber, and Ciccone 2011). Using the process of inquiry, evidence, and innovation shared by SoTL and assessment will help faculty accomplish the goal of enhanced student learning. To this end, a cultural shift must occur. Typically, faculty teach courses, design SoTL research, create assessments, and test pedagogies in isolation. We encourage faculty to break down the artificial boundaries between courses, between faculty, and between teaching and research in order to highlight connections and contributions across these student-centered endeavors. In other words, we must move from pedagogical solitude to collective engagement. Rather than individual instructors focusing on their own classes in isolated silos, faculty need to work collaboratively and collectively to create the best learning experience for students.

SoTL Can Enhance Student Learning

Instructors commonly reflect upon how well students are learning relative to how they (instructors) are teaching the course material. When students do not appear to grasp the main concepts and skills of a course, instructors often search the literature to learn about teaching techniques other instructors have found useful and apply the new approach in their own class. Next, instructors often informally assess whether students' learning of the material improved. This is the process of scholarly teaching (Richlin 2001). Scholarly teachers actively seek out methods to improve student learning and observe how student learning changes based on classroom experiences.

Scholarly teachers engage in informal inquiry for the direct purpose of enhancing their own students' learning. These efforts should be lauded, for they provide the first steps of innovation toward the continual improvement of teaching and learning. As illustrated in Figure 2.1, scholarly teaching satisfies individual curiosities for the betterment of an individual group of students. Yet, it is the isolated nature of these experiences that limits the impact.

NEW DIRECTIONS FOR TEACHING AND LEARNING • DOI: 10.1002/tl

Figure 2.1. Scholarly Teaching

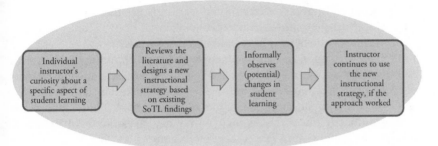

Figure 2.2. SoTL Research

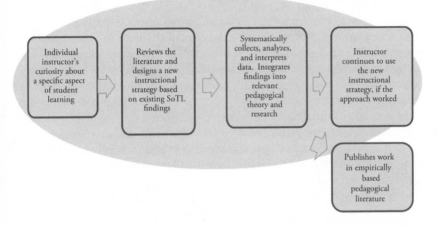

To broaden the impact of new teaching strategies, we encourage faculty to take it to the next level through participation in SoTL. SoTL takes an applied approach by framing and systematically investigating questions related to student learning with the goals of improving student learning in specific classes and contributing to scholarly literature (Hutchings and Shulman 1999).

Similar to scholarly teaching, SoTL inquiry is often motivated by an instructor's curiosity about how students are learning in his/her classes (Bass 1999). The difference is that faculty who employ SoTL methods apply the systematic inquiry and evidence processes found in all areas of research. Following examination of existing research and theory, a SoTL scholar develops a research question, designs a research method to answer the question, collects data, interprets the results, and publishes findings (see Figure 2.2).

Teaching practices derived from SoTL must be utilized for the findings to positively impact student learning (Potter and Kustra 2011). SoTL researchers typically continue to use the innovative approach to impact their own students' learning. Making SoTL work publicly available broadens the scope of impact so that scholarly teachers at other institutions can utilize empirically supported practices and techniques to enhance their students' learning. Innovation occurs when scholars learn from the experiences of others, reflect upon their own practice, and synthesize the findings with their own new ideas and approaches to generate novel, inspiring pedagogies. The impact of most SoTL findings tends to be at the classroom level. To broaden the impact beyond the classroom level, McKinney and Jarvis (2009) emphasize that SoTL researchers should also explicitly link their results or conclusions to program-level interventions and institutional-level educational opportunities.

Assessment Can Enhance Student Learning

When the assessment movement first hit higher education, the primary purpose of assessment on college campuses was to answer calls for institutional effectiveness and accountability (Ewell 2009). Driven by accreditation, the focus was on whether students met specified standards for learning outcomes. Many faculty were offended by the public demand to justify their existence and prove not only that students were learning but also what they were learning.

Fortunately, innovative faculty and assessment practitioners identified how to evolve assessment beyond documentation of student performance to include using the assessment process and findings to help faculty better understand and improve student learning (Angelo 1995). In this sense, faculty turned the lemons of assessment into lemonade, fashioning a potentially empty bureaucratic process into a process that could feed and support their efforts to enhance student learning.

When faculty own their assessment practices, it is far more likely that the empirical evidence derived from their research will be used to improve student learning in their courses and academic programs. Faculty are much more likely to engage in assessment efforts when the focus is on how they can enhance student learning through their teaching and curricular design efforts, rather than solely focusing on accountability issues. When assessment findings are applied to an academic program, faculty can better understand how the cohesive, integrative collection of courses that define the curriculum facilitates student learning en masse.

Figure 2.3 illustrates the assessment cycle. Following examination of the curriculum, the faculty as a group select a useful assessment question, collect and analyze data, interpret the results, and reflect upon the data to determine whether or not students learned what the faculty wanted them to learn. Then, based on their interpretation of the results, modifications are made to teaching practices, courses, and/or the design of the curriculum. Compared to the SoTL process, notice the shift in focus from a SoTL

Figure 2.3. Academic Program Assessment Cycle

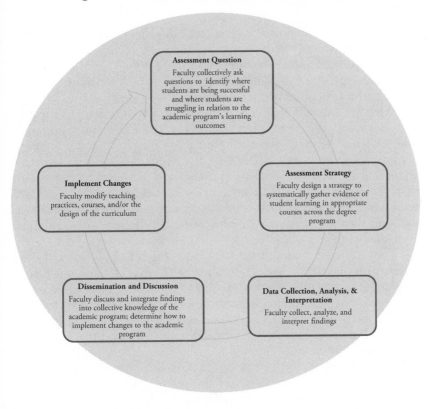

researcher asking an independently derived pedagogical question for an isolated course to faculty collectively considering student learning within an academic program.

Well-designed assessment efforts can help faculty identify authentic points of success that can be used to celebrate student learning within an academic program and discover where students are having difficulties in order to make improvements. Using assessment findings to identify where students are struggling helps faculty determine where they should focus their improvement efforts.

As instructors design learning opportunities for strategic improvements, they should be informed by theoretical, research-based knowledge found in SoTL publications. SoTL literature provides a plethora of empirically based strategies for bolstering student learning. Scholarly teachers can utilize the strategies in their classes. A SoTL researcher can then systematically test the impact of the innovative approach. SoTL research questions that are informed by assessment findings within a program increase the impact beyond an individual course to affect an entire academic program.

Coordinating SoTL and Assessment Efforts to Enhance Student Learning

Coordinated assessment and SoTL efforts can help faculty discover where students are having difficulties and systematically investigate whether an innovative pedagogy improves student learning. When coordinating SoTL and assessment, you will want to increase the impact of your research by working with colleagues in your department.

What are you and your colleagues curious about relative to your students' learning? Where are your students struggling? Upon reflection of your students' learning, what innovative teaching technique or unique learning design do you think could facilitate your students' learning? How would improvements in students' learning in your course facilitate learning in subsequent courses? Consider what knowledge and skills your students have developed prior to entering your course, and what knowledge and skills they will need to use in the courses that follow yours within the academic program.

Conversations among instructors regarding the application of disciplinary pedagogical changes can result in SoTL research questions that are meaningful to the entire academic program. Upon creation of the question, degree program faculty can collectively review the literature and develop innovative instructional approaches tailored to the talents and needs of their program. Data collection occurs when the new assignment or approach is used across sections of a course or across courses. Upon considering SoTL and assessment findings, instructors can consider the greater context of their program in identifying how well the new instructional techniques improved student learning. Faculty members can then collaborate and coordinate where, when, and how often to implement program-level instructional changes. Through collective engagement, faculty can identify where in their program the innovative teaching practices will have the greatest impact.

Let us explore an example of coordinated assessment and SoTL efforts. A disciplinary "bottleneck" in learning occurs when a majority of students are unable to master a specific disciplinary problem, concept, or process, and therefore cannot proceed to fully grasp higher-level integrative concepts of the discipline (Pace and Middendorf 2004). A common bottleneck in psychology is that students fail to understand that psychology is a science. Many beginning students are focused on the interesting psychological concepts and principles that they are learning without fully understanding the scientific foundation that generated the content. If students do not grasp this foundational concept, their ability to truly comprehend psychology is thwarted. SoTL is precisely the tool of inquiry that can identify how to unplug bottlenecks, yet exploring this research question across courses within your degree program can raise this SoTL question to have meaningful and lasting impact across your degree program.

In designing a research question from this area, our SoTL questions are (1) where are bottlenecks occurring in the learning across our discipline, (2) how are instructors across our department approaching these bottlenecks, and (3) how can we improve our students' learning at these points in our program? Rather than approaching the SoTL question in isolation without consideration of how the courses work together to facilitate student learning, we encourage instructors to examine the question and identify how this important area of teaching and learning impacts the learning outcomes of the entire program.

Instructors can look to SoTL literature for help. What can we learn from the literature about navigating students through a particular bottleneck? What successful pedagogies complement approaches used in the degree program? In many disciplines, scholars have identified ways in which instructors can break down the disciplinary ways of thinking to train students to think like professionals in that field of study (for example, Gurung, Chick, and Haynie 2009). Exploring how others in the discipline approached this challenge and brainstorming mechanisms with your colleagues on how these methods can be adapted to fulfill the specific learning goals of your degree program transforms this SoTL question into a highly meaningful assessment question within your degree program. When coordinated SoTL and assessment questions focus specifically on areas to improve student learning within an academic program, it is far more likely that the results can and will be used in courses and across the program.

The development and testing of the new teaching method would then be carried out across at least one course, perhaps across multiple courses, wherein bottlenecks occur. Following the collection of data, we encourage faculty to work collectively to review their assessment and SoTL findings. Discuss your findings with your colleagues and hear about their experiences in the classroom, and how these relate to the data collected from assessments of students learning. These important conversations are critical for teasing out whether the change in teaching method made the difference and whether the assessment selected to test the change is valid. To obtain the greatest impacts from the research study, we must remember that coordination and cohesion across courses within a degree program are essential to raise the degree program from a set of independent courses developed by individual faculty to a product that is greater than the sum of its parts. Figure 2.4 illustrates the example of coordinating SoTL and assessment efforts to identify bottlenecks in a degree program and enhance student learning.

When considering SoTL and assessment findings, we recommend that faculty members collaborate and coordinate where, when, and how often learning outcomes will be taught and how knowledge and skills will be integrated appropriately across the curriculum. Through collective

Figure 2.4. Coordinating SoTL and Assessment to Identify Bottlenecks

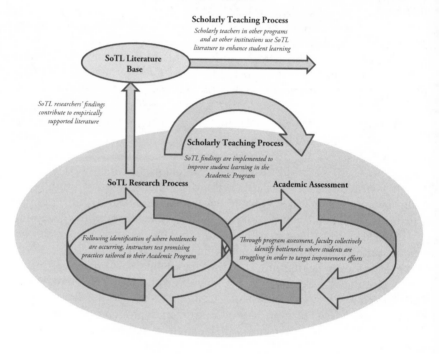

engagement, faculty can identify where in their program the innovative teaching practices will have the greatest impact. By discussing coordinated SoTL and assessment results with colleagues we:

- learn whether our colleagues have similar experiences in their courses;
- improve our understanding of patterns of student learning across courses;
- identify, collectively, where and how to make improvements;
- use empirical evidence to guide strategic teaching and learning improvements; and
- create opportunities for new SoTL and assessment questions (Dunn et al. 2013).

To broaden the impact that SoTL and assessment can have independently, faculty need to think collectively and coordinate their research efforts. As we engage in conversations with colleagues, we can identify how to use the SoTL findings to impact student learning through the development and application of new teaching techniques and approaches. Strategically designed learning opportunities that are grounded in one's own program and focused on explicitly stated learning goals empower scholarly teachers to enhance student learning.

New Directions for Teaching and Learning • DOI: 10.1002/tl

Figure 2.5. Coordinated Scholarly Teaching, SoTL Research, and Academic Assessment Efforts

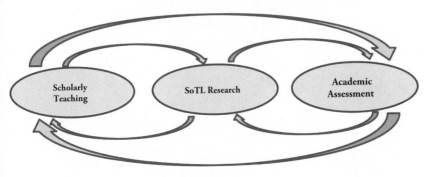

Moving Forward

As illustrated in Figure 2.5, to maximally enhance student learning, scholarly teaching, SoTL research, and assessment processes should be coordinated. Scholarly teachers depend on SoTL findings to improve student learning. Using the assessment process, faculty collectively identify specific areas where students are struggling, which leads to targeted areas for SoTL inquiry. Based on conversations with colleagues and exploration of the literature, SoTL researchers systematically test innovative approaches to address the problem areas. Utilization of empirically supported pedagogies derived from the SoTL process enhances student learning within academic programs. Dissemination of SoTL work feeds the literature base that scholarly teachers depend upon.

Moving Forward

This volume will provide you with the tools necessary to conduct a rigorous, systematic investigation of the impact your teaching has on students' learning. Documentation and publication of SoTL work is an important endeavor as they increase our collective knowledge of empirically supported pedagogy.

To enhance student learning, faculty must utilize the evidence gathered from their SoTL research and assessment to inform practices in our classrooms, programs, and institutions. SoTL and assessment provide the processes of inquiry, evidence, and innovation that serve as the foundation for continual improvement. Faculty need to lead the institutional integration of these valuable processes by building bridges and engaging in collaborative inquiry.

Help shape the future by talking with your colleagues about student learning. From your assessment findings, identify where your students are struggling and systematically test innovative approaches that target those areas. Share your SoTL research findings with your colleagues so that student learning in your program can be enhanced. Publish your work through the peer-review process so that all of us in the research/teaching community can improve. Join the community of teacher scholars and cultivate a culture of continual improvement in your program, institution, and higher education, in general.

References

Angelo, T. A. 1995. "Reassessing (and Defining) Assessment." *The AAHE Bulletin* 48 (2): 7–9.

Bass, R. 1999. "The Scholarship of Teaching: What's the Problem?" *Inventio: Creative Thinking About Learning and Teaching* 1 (1). http://www2.okcu.edu/cetl/randybass.pdf.

Dunn, D. S., S. C. Baker, C. M. Mehrotra, R. E. Landrum, and M. A. McCarthy. 2013. *Assessing Teaching and Learning in Psychology: Current and Future Perspectives*. Belmont, CA: Wadsworth.

Ewell, P. T. 2009. *Assessment, Accountability, and Improvement: Revisiting the Tension*. Urbana-Champaign: National Institute for Learning Outcomes Assessment (NILOA), University of Illinois.

Gurung, R. A. R., N. Chick, and A. Haynie, eds. 2009. *Exploring Signature Pedagogies: Approaches to Teaching Disciplinary Habits of Mind*. Sterling, VA: Stylus.

Hutchings, P., M. T. Huber, and A. Ciccone. 2011. *The Scholarship of Teaching Reconsidered: Institutional Integration and Impact*. San Francisco: Jossey-Bass.

Hutchings, P., and L. S. Shulman. 1999. "The Scholarship of Teaching: New Elaborations, New Developments." *Change* 31: 11–15.

McKinney, K., and P. Jarvis. 2009. "Beyond Lines on the CV: Faculty Applications of their Scholarship of Teaching and Learning Research." *International Journal for the Scholarship of Teaching and Learning* 3 (1). http://digitalcommons.georgiasouthern.edu/cgi/viewcontent.cgi?article=1124&context=int_jtl.

Pace, D., and J. Middendorf. 2004. "Helping Students Learn Disciplinary Ways of Thinking." In *Decoding the Disciplines: Helping Students Learn Disciplinary Ways of Thinking*, New Directions for Teaching and Learning, no. 98, edited by D. Pace and J. Middendorf, 1–12. San Francisco: Jossey-Bass.

Potter, M. K., and E. Kustra. 2011. "The Relationship between Scholarly Teaching and SoTL: Models, Distinctions, and Clarifications." *International Journal for the Scholarship of Teaching and Learning* 5 (1): 1–18.

Richlin, L. 2001. "Scholarly Teaching and the Scholarship of Teaching." In *Scholarship Revisited: Perspectives on the Scholarship of Teaching*, edited by C. Kreber, 57–68. San Francisco: Jossey-Bass.

K. Laurie Dickson *is a professor of psychology and the associate vice provost of the Office of Curriculum, Learning Design, and Academic Assessment, Northern Arizona University.*

Melinda M. Treml *is the associate director of the Office of Curriculum, Learning Design, and Academic Assessment, Northern Arizona University.*

3

This chapter discusses how to improve validity in SoTL studies through generating appropriate measures and using designs that examine causality between an activity and students' performance.

Designing SoTL Studies—Part I: Validity

Robert A. Bartsch

The Scholarship of Teaching and Learning (SoTL) includes interesting and important research areas including motivational factors of performance (e.g., Pintrich 2004), identifying exemplary instructors (e.g., Theall and Feldman 2007), and factors in student-instructor relationships (e.g., Wilson, Wilson, and Legg 2012). Another important and possibly most prominent area of SoTL research examines effectiveness of classroom activities (Wilson-Doenges and Gurung 2013). Instructors make changes to their courses with the goal of improving academic quality. These changes may be minor, such as adding a small ten-minute classroom demonstration to teach a specific concept, or major, such as adding new technology or redesigning an entire class. Instructors use these activities in an attempt to improve knowledge content, skills, and attitudes (Tomcho and Foels 2008). This chapter focuses on assessing the effectiveness of these classroom activities. In addition, many of the hints and strategies presented can be applied to other SoTL areas.

Instructors practicing scholarly teaching want to know whether their activities are effective. We puzzle over why they should work, reflect on what happened, and perhaps, glance at grades to see if they worked (Smith 2008). Unfortunately, sometimes these subjective observations are not enough. For example, after lecturing on social influence, I tell students that they need to use ten influence techniques to make mock arguments telling me why their grade should be raised. Students enjoy the task, and with the active participation and application, I believe students learn more, but I must admit, I do not know if that happens. Perhaps the task is too easy. Perhaps students do not generalize this activity to other situations. I am not sure. I am violating Smith's (2008) recommendation to be intentional and systematic in evaluating my teaching materials.

It is important to document and objectively test our SoTL research questions (Schwartz and Gurung 2012; Smith 2008, 2012). When we make our systematic observations, we want to do good research. Good research

NEW DIRECTIONS FOR TEACHING AND LEARNING, no. 136, Winter 2013 © 2013 Wiley Periodicals, Inc.
Published online in Wiley Online Library (wileyonlinelibrary.com) • DOI: 10.1002/tl.20073

provides evidence supporting or refuting hypotheses such as my social influence activity leads to greater student learning. Poor research does not provide an opportunity to support or refute the hypothesis. For example, I might measure my students' knowledge of social influence tactics after my activity. The students may score very high. Hooray! However, I do not know what their knowledge was before my activity. Students may have already known the material and the activity did not help. I have neither supported nor refuted the hypothesis that my activity improved student learning. My research was not useful.

Construct and Internal Validity

To be useful, SoTL studies need to be valid. Validity refers to the "approximate truth of an inference" (Shadish, Cook, and Campbell 2002, 34). If a study's methods are valid, we have confidence that the conclusions we make are accurate. Unfortunately, assessing the validity of a study is not an easy yes/no evaluation. Also, multiple types of validity exist, with each type asking a different question. Construct validity asks whether we can make inferences based on how well we have measured or manipulated our variables (Shadish, Cook, and Campbell 2002) or "Am I measuring what I say I am measuring?" Construct validity is important in all studies. Without construct validity, we cannot say that we have a good measure. For example, I have heard instructors who grade lengthy essays joke that they will save time and assign grades by weight. Weight is a measure of quality of the essay, but not a good one. A study that used this measure would have low construct validity.

Internal validity asks whether one can establish if the treatment caused the outcome (Shadish, Cook, and Campbell 2002) or "Did this cause that?" Only studies with a causal claim care about internal validity. For example, if I wanted to know what students knew after my social influence activity, I do not care about internal validity, but if I wanted to know if my activity increased their knowledge, I do care about internal validity. Without internal validity I cannot say that my activity *caused* higher levels of student learning.

Hypotheses for causal studies can be thought of in terms of independent and dependent variables. An independent variable is the cause, and the dependent variable is the effect (Fan 2010). The researcher controls or manipulates the independent variable. For example, a researcher may provide one section of class a teaching activity but not a comparable section. The presence or absence of the manipulation, typically a teaching activity, is the independent variable or what I call the *treatment*. The dependent variable is not in the researcher's control and is always measured, and I refer to it as the *assessment*. The assessment can measure learning, skills, attitudes, or whatever the researcher hopes the treatment changes in the students. Therefore, a simple research hypothesis takes the following form: *the treatment (independent variable) improves students on the assessment (dependent variable)*. When researchers are interested in causality, three major problems related to construct and internal validity are possible:

- The assessment was not measured well. (construct validity)
- The treatment was not manipulated well. (construct validity)
- Something other than the treatment caused change in the assessment. (internal validity)

As a side note, because instructors are conducting studies when they do SoTL, I refer to these instructors as researchers throughout the chapter.

I have some general warnings when evaluating construct and internal validity. First, a study does not have absolute validity or absolutely no validity (Shadish, Cook, and Campbell 2002). The level of validity relates to the confidence in the conclusions we make, and that confidence is on a continuum. Second, just because a study has construct validity does not mean it has internal validity, and just because a study has internal validity does not mean it has construct validity. In fact, construct validity of the treatment and the assessment is a separate evaluation. Third, just because the results of a study come out as predicted does not mean that the study has either construct or internal validity. Construct and internal validity are determined primarily by the methods used and not the results. Therefore, researchers should know if they are doing valid research as they design their study well before data collection begins.

Good Measures Lead to High Construct Validity

Because it is important for all studies, I will first focus on evaluating construct validity and suggestions for improving it. To discuss construct validity, we need to understand the terms *construct* and *operational definition*. A construct is a "concept, model, or schematic idea" (Shadish, Cook, and Campbell 2002, 506) and represents the global notion of the measure. For example, student learning, student anxiety, and student enjoyment are all constructs. The specific method of measuring a construct is called the operational definition. For example, an operational definition of student learning may be the grade on the final class exam and an operational definition of statistics anxiety may be a score on the Statistics Anxiety Rating Scale (Hanna, Shevlin, and Dempster 2008).

For any construct, researchers can choose many, many possible operational definitions. For example, if we wanted to measure student-instructor relationship, we could use established measures such as the Student Engagement Instrument (Appleton et al. 2006) and the Student Trust Scale (Adams and Forsyth 2009). Also, researchers could ask students "How warm or cool do you feel toward your instructor?" on a hundred-point thermometer scale or ask several interrelated Likert-scale questions. The researcher could also make ratings based on direct observation of the students and teachers. Some measurements are poor (i.e., the operational definition does not align with the construct) and some are good (i.e., the operational definition does align with the construct). It is nearly impossible to get a perfect fit between the operational definition and construct. Each measure will have some error, but the more one can minimize the error, the greater the construct validity.

Creating valid measures sounds easy but it can be challenging. I recommend spending a good amount of time developing good measures. In the next section, I describe several common strategies to improve construct validity of the assessment. Not all strategies work in all situations. Also, to further complicate matters, some of these suggestions can be contradictory. They are contradictory because creating a benefit with one type of validity can have unintended consequences for other parts of the study. In addition, sometimes validity cannot be improved due to practical or ethical considerations.

Measure Learning Directly When the Goal Is to Measure Learning. I argue that the most important construct in SoTL research is student learning. Unfortunately, studies that attempt to measure student learning may measure student enjoyment or perceived learning (Bartsch 2006). It is much easier to ask students whether they enjoyed an activity or thought they learned something rather than developing and administering a measure of actual student learning. Unfortunately, using enjoyment or perceived learning as a measure of actual learning is problematic.

Student enjoyment does not necessarily match with student learning (e.g., Bartsch and Cobern 2003). Although students may learn more from an activity that is enjoyable than a similar activity that is not enjoyable, all enjoyable instructional techniques do not necessarily lead to student learning. I still remember in grade school a weeklong lesson on Clyde Clunk's Birthday, a made-up character for the week. I thought the lessons were fun, but I did not learn much. In fact, material that challenges students may not be as enjoyable as less challenging material. If a researcher wants to measure student enjoyment, then it is appropriate to ask questions regarding enjoyment; however, if a researcher wants to measure student learning, then enjoyment should not be used as a substitute.

Similarly, sometimes teachers ask students whether they perceive they learned the material. Asking students their perception of their learning is quicker than testing for learning itself, but this type of measure may not relate to retention of course material (Kornell and Bjork 2008; Simon and Bjork 2001; Wesp and Miele 2008). As with enjoyment, a challenging assignment may promote learning, but because it is challenging, students may not feel as fluent with their performance and may rate their perceived learning lower compared to students who had a less challenging assignment.

If researchers want to measure learning, they should directly measure learning. Researchers can use a variety of forms to measure learning including but not limited to multiple choice, true/false, short answers, and essays. Gurung and Landrum (2012) present a large list of assessments categorized by behavioral-based vs. perception-based and objective vs. subjective measures.

Measure Learning through Student Learning Objectives. Not only should researchers measure learning but they should also examine student learning objectives and align these with the study's assessment. Learning objectives can include conceptual knowledge, skills including critical thinking, and attitudes and habits of mind (Gurung and Landrum 2012; Suskie 2009). If the learning objective includes advanced ways of learning such as analysis, synthesis, and evaluation, then the assessment should not comprise lower levels of learning such as recognizing simple facts. If established assignments are used for the assessment, the scoring on the assignment needs to be associated with the student objectives and no other factors such as penalties for late assignments or improper formatting. Therefore, class assignments that are used as measures may need separate scoring for a SoTL project.

Have Clear Questions and Answer Choices. Any time a student answers a question, the questions and answer choices should be clear. As instructors we know if we put a vague question or confusing answer choices on an exam, then we do not have an exam that accurately tests our students. In other words, our measure of student learning has reduced construct validity. Similarly, with any research measure, whether it is a survey, test, or essay, vague questions will likely cause increases in random error and will reduce the construct validity.

One strategy to avoid this problem is to have another instructor or researcher proof the assessment. An alternate strategy is to conduct a pilot test with other students or teaching assistants to make sure they understand the questions. Think-aloud protocols (Dillman 2000), in which helpers state aloud what they are thinking as they go through questions, can highlight additional problems with clarity.

Use Established Scales to Measure Student Attitudes and Personality. Some studies measure student attitudes. For example, in a recent issue of the *International Journal for the Scholarship of Teaching and Learning*, researchers used many measures including comfort and familiarity with lecture, student satisfaction, communication apprehension, interest in engaging in research, learning approach preference, and opinions about specific learning activities. Researchers do not have to reinvent the wheel when measuring these constructs. Rather, I encourage researchers to use already developed measures of attitudes and personality. One may even find established measures of student learning. The *Directory of Unpublished Experimental Mental Measures* (Goldman and Mitchell 2007) provides a large number of noncommercial scales present in the literature including measures of test anxiety, classroom behavior, and college/university attitudes. College and university libraries may also have access to the PsycTESTS database from the American Psychological Association, which also includes a variety of developed measures, many of which can be used at no cost for research purposes.

Know How to Score the Measure.   Once one has a measure, one needs to know how to score it. How one scores the measure should be known before data collection. Too often, researchers might collect data, but not understand how the data will turn into scores on the variables they want to measure. Although this is acceptable for qualitative approaches such as ethnographic research, it is not a good practice for quantitative research. If one uses an established measure, the article describing it should provide scoring instructions. If it is the researcher's own measure, instructions for scoring should be documented. In addition, if one scores a subjective measure such as an essay, I recommend researchers use a rubric and have two people score the measure. Raters should spend time training together so they will score similarly. With two raters, a researcher can examine inter-observer reliability (Gall, Gall, and Borg 2007). Raters should have similar scores and if they are, then the measure has high inter-observer reliability. If scores are not similar, then more training on scoring is needed. If one has problems developing questions, answers, or scoring, I recommend looking for campus experts, reference books, or chapters in methodology textbooks on survey construction.

Minimize Participant Expectancies.   Students in SoTL research may know that they are being measured, and this knowledge can affect their responses (Shadish, Cook, and Campbell 2002), decreasing construct validity. For example, knowing that they are being observed, some students may try harder (e.g., the Hawthorne effect; Shadish, Cook, and Campbell 2002). In other cases, students often realize that the instructor wants them to learn from the treatment. Consequently, with perceived learning measures, students will state that they did learn—either to please the instructor or make themselves look better in the eyes of the instructor. Similar problems occur with student enjoyment measures.

Using existing class assignments minimizes problems with participant expectancies. In these cases, students may not even know that they are in a study. Archival measures can also be used such as attendance and past GPA. Other methods to combat participant expectancies involve using anonymous measures or creating a cover story that misleads students from the true nature of the study (Dunn 2009).

Minimize Researcher Expectancies.   Researchers can also be biased by expectancies (Shadish, Cook, and Campbell 2002), also decreasing construct validity. For example, if I knew an essay came from one of my best students, I may unconsciously make ratings (even with a rubric) that are in line with my expectations about the student. If a measure has subjective elements (e.g., essays), it is useful to have a researcher who is blind to the participant, that is, a researcher who does not know who the student is, score the measure.

Determine Whether to Use Graded or Ungraded Measures.   In developing an appropriate measure of student learning, researchers will have to decide whether to use graded or ungraded measures. Graded and ungraded assignments have advantages and disadvantages. Graded assignments do not add any additional time to the class. Also, because the grade counts, students are motivated to do well on them. Ungraded tasks or assignments have their own advantages. First, ungraded assignments reduce ethical concerns. Second, ungraded assignments can be tailored more specifically to the student learning outcome. Combining some elements of both graded and ungraded assignments, researchers can use graded assignments but have a separate scoring system for the SoTL project that more closely aligns with the student learning outcome.

Determine Whether to Use Multiple Operational Definitions.   Researchers have the option to use multiple operational definitions to measure a construct. For example, if a researcher wants to measure student learning, the researcher could do so with both an exam and a separate essay assignment. Stehle, Spinath, and Kadmon (2012) wanted to predict student learning from student evaluations of teaching. They used multiple measures of medical student learning: a multiple-choice test and an interaction with a simulated patient. They found opposite results for the two operational definitions of student learning, which led to a more nuanced understanding of the relationship between teaching evaluations and student learning. Using multiple operational definitions often adds to the construct validity of the study, but the study takes more time to complete.

Use an Additional Post-Test to Investigate Long-Term Effects.   Many times, researchers are interested in whether any change lasts. With many designs, a post-test can be added (e.g., at the end of the semester) to determine long-term change. With this addition, a researcher can have evidence that any changes persisted over a longer period. However, during the long term, other factors such as new instruction or studying or even changes in student maturity may cloud interpretation of results. Most long-term assessments may provide some support for the idea of long-term change, but generally these results should be treated with caution.

Good Differences between Conditions Improve Construct Validity

In the last section, I discussed how good measurement is important. That discussion focused on assessments such as measures of student learning, student attitudes, and so on. These assessments concerned effects. Researchers are also concerned with construct validity of the treatment (i.e., the independent variable). For example, in a study on whether using electronic classroom response systems or "clickers" causes increases in student learning, we are concerned with not only how we measure student learning but also how we manipulate clicker use.

I will call the condition with the treatment the *treatment condition*. Others may refer to it as an experimental condition or as an intervention. The condition without the treatment is the *control condition*. Just as the assessment needs to be measured well to ensure construct validity, the treatment needs to be manipulated well to ensure construct validity. Oftentimes this manipulation means some students are in a treatment condition and others are in a control condition. For example, one class uses clickers and the other class does not. Alternatively, the same students are assessed at different times in the treatment and control conditions. In this example, students would have some classes with clickers and other classes without clickers and be assessed after each.

In both cases, how the treatment and control conditions are operationally defined should align with the construct of the independent variable. Just as some measurements are good and some are poor, some treatment manipulations are good and some are poor. The next section describes some strategies for manipulating the treatment to ensure construct validity.

Only Manipulate the Treatment.   The only difference between the conditions should be the treatment. Other variables that are also different between conditions but are not the treatment are called *confounds* (Shadish, Cook, and Campbell 2002). For example, suppose I used clickers in the classroom but took longer to cover the material compared to a nonclicker control condition. In this case, time spent is a confound. Any difference on student learning between conditions could be caused by the clicker use or the amount of time studied or both. We do not know. As another example, Anthis (2011) pointed out a common confound in clicker research is that in the clicker condition students are exposed to additional questions. Perhaps simply asking the additional questions causes the improved performance and not the use of the clickers themselves.

To determine construct validity, treatments need specific operational definitions. For example, it would be inadequate to say that I used clickers in the treatment condition, did not use clickers in the control condition, and offered no additional details. Other information that needs to be known includes the type of clickers, how the use of clickers was introduced to students, how often clickers were used, what types of questions were asked with clickers, and what the instructor did when students responded. Basically, anything that can affect the results and cause a difference between students in the treatment and control conditions needs to be documented.

What happens in any control condition is also important. In the current example, simply saying that the control condition did not involve clickers would not be enough. This information also needs to be stated, and several possibilities exist. First, the control condition has no instruction. Second, the control condition includes instruction unrelated to the assessment. Both of these options can bias the treatment condition because students who receive the treatment may have additional instruction on the topic to be assessed. This additional instruction and not the specific treatment itself may cause the change.

A third possibility is that the control condition receives relevant instruction but not with clickers. This type of design is recommended because it directly compares the treatment to instruction that normally occurs. Anthis (2011) used a fourth possibility, which is also recommended. In her study, the control condition was the same as the treatment condition except that the technology was removed. Specifically, students saw the same questions, but answered by raising their hands. The instructor told students in both conditions that they could copy the questions down.

Beware of Using Different Sections.   Classes are a social space, and students and the instructor are interdependent. This interdependence means different sections of classes will have differences even if the instructor, lectures, and assignments are the same. Students from different classes will ask different questions. A different tone may develop. Students will help each other understand. Unfortunately for researchers, all these differences become potential confounds when comparing one class with another (Grauerholz and Main 2013). Therefore, construct validity of the treatment is questionable in any design that compares one section of a class with another, because classes will differ in more than just the presence or absence of the treatment.

Splitting a single class into two groups minimizes this concern, as students in the two conditions would have shared much of the same social space until the split occurs. In fact, if possible, I recommend splitting each class rather than having one class as the treatment condition and the other class as a control condition. Furthermore, if students in a split class can be randomly assigned to condition, internal validity will increase.

Minimize Participant Expectancies.   Not only do participant expectancies affect assessment measurement as discussed earlier but also problems with expectancies can affect the treatment manipulation. If students know that multiple conditions exist, they may be concerned about their benefits or detriments or try harder or less hard because of their condition. If conditions consist of different classes, students are less likely to know. If both conditions exist in a single class, students should be blind to condition, meaning that they do not know which condition they are in (Shadish, Cook, and Campbell 2002). For example, if a researcher wanted to investigate whether humor on an exam leads to higher scores, the researcher could create two similar looking exams but one has humor added to it. Students would likely not realize the different conditions (unless some started laughing in the middle of the exam). Researchers can also separate the class into two halves and keep them apart until the study is completed (e.g., Smith 2008). In addition, a cover story to disguise the study's hypothesis can be used.

Minimize Researcher Expectancies.   If possible, the instructor interacting with the students should be blind to condition. Otherwise, the researcher may behave differently to the groups because of the researcher's expectation of what should happen. For example, if a researcher wanted to determine if adding scaffolding to an essay assignment led to better essays, the researcher could have another instructor score the essays. The scorer would not know whether an essay came from control instructions or the scaffolding instructions. If the researcher cannot be blind to condition, the researcher should try to be as consistent as possible when interacting with students in the two conditions including using scripts to keep interactions the same.

Good Comparisons between Conditions Improve Internal Validity

To determine if a treatment condition caused a change on the assessment, researchers compare students in a treatment condition with a control condition. We can make between-participants comparisons or within-participants comparisons. In between-participants comparisons, each student is in a single condition. In a within-participants design (sometimes called within-groups or repeated-measures), students are in all conditions.

I discuss three types of designs used to infer causality between the treatment and assessment: between-participants, within-participants, and pre-test/post-test. All involve creating comparison groups, but in different ways. Each design has its own advantages and disadvantages, and each has different strategies for maximizing internal validity. Table 3.1 outlines these different designs.

Compare Students to Other Students: Between-Participants Designs. The first type of design uses a between-participants approach, comparing students who receive the treatment to similar students in the control condition who did not receive the treatment. To achieve internal validity in this type of design, the students in the treatment condition need to be equivalent to students in the control condition. When students are not equivalent, selection bias occurs (Shadish, Cook, and Campbell 2002). Differences between the two groups may cause differences in the assessment. For example, suppose one class used clickers and another was the control condition. Even if the treatment class scored higher than the control class on the assessment, confounds are likely. Students in the treatment class may have better motivation or more initial knowledge of the topic.

Use Random Assignment to Equalize Groups. A main method to equalize students in the treatment and control conditions is to randomly assign students to condition. Random assignment occurs when each student has an equal chance of being placed in each condition. Random assignment roughly equalizes groups on each and every variable at the same time except for the treatment (Braver, Moser, and Thoemmes 2010). Students who are high on one characteristic (e.g., motivation to study) are likely to be split between the two conditions, and students who are low on that

Table 3.1. Different Types of Comparisons in Research Designs

	Between-Participants	Within-Participants	Pre-Test/Post-Test
How comparison works	Students in control condition compared to students in treatment condition	All students in both control and treatment conditions	Students receive both pre-test (control) and post-test (treatment condition)
Strengths	No carryover effects from multiple treatments; no instrumentation or testing effects from multiple assessments	No selection bias; greater statistical power	No selection bias; greater statistical power
Weaknesses	Selection bias if do not use random assignment; many differences if groups are separate (e.g., two separate classes); lower statistical power	Instrumentation and testing effects; carryover effects	Instrumentation and testing effects; other confounds that occur between assessments
Improve internal validity by	Random assignment of students to conditions; adding covariates	Counterbalancing	Increase number of pre-tests/post-tests; add separate control condition that does not receive treatment; using alternative measures for assessment

characteristic are also likely to be split between the conditions. Therefore, on average, the conditions should be similar. Not only are conditions equalized on that characteristic but they are also equalized on every other characteristic. The only difference remaining is the treatment, and the treatment is the only cause of any assessment difference.

Use Covariates to Equalize Groups.   Another strategy to decrease selection bias is to use covariates. Covariates are variables other than the treatment that also predict the assessment. Covariates can be statistically equalized between the groups, making the groups statistically similar. For example, Barak and Dori (2004) wanted to study how project-based learning would improve student learning. However, the course instructor would not permit random assignment to project-based learning or traditional assignments. Rather, the instructor only allowed students to self-select. Self-selection causes a host of confounds through selection bias because students who volunteer for the problem-based learning may be different from students who do not volunteer. The confounds and not the treatment could cause any observed difference in final exam grades. To reduce the selection bias, the researchers used a covariate, university entry level grades. Researchers used statistics to equalize the groups on the covariate. In the resulting analysis, university entry level grades can no longer be used to explain differences between the conditions. Unfortunately, other variables can still be confounds. Nevertheless, using one or two important covariates can increase the internal validity of a study. As an additional advantage, covariates often increase statistical power (Shadish, Cook, and Campbell 2002); that is, if the treatment produces an effect, the researcher is more likely to find it.

Know How Students Differ between Conditions.   A third strategy to minimize selection bias is to document how similar or different students are in each condition. Researchers examine each group on variables that may affect the results. These variables often include demographic characteristics (e.g., age and year in school) and past performance (e.g., SAT/ACT and last semester's GPA). Small differences indicate that the groups are equivalent and can be compared. Large differences between the groups are a potential confound. Unfortunately, just like covariates, it is impossible to examine all relevant variables.

Compare Students to Themselves: Within-Participants and Pre-Test/Post-Test Studies.   One weakness of between-participants comparisons is that if students from the treatment and control conditions are not similar, selection bias occurs. Researchers can avoid selection bias by having the same students in both control and treatment conditions (Dunn 2009). Students are compared to themselves. One cannot get more similar than that.

I describe two different designs: within-participants and pre-test/post-test. In within-participants designs, researchers expose students to multiple treatments and students are assessed after each treatment. For example, in one of my studies (Bartsch and Cobern 2003), we examined whether students remembered more from PowerPoint presentations that had slides with no pictures, slides with relevant pictures, or slides with irrelevant pictures. We presented all three treatments to each student in the study.

A within-participants study can have any number of treatments. Because students are exposed to each condition, students need more time to complete the study compared to between-participants designs. Within-participants designs do not work well when the treatment has a long-term effect on the assessment, known as a carryover effect (Shadish, Cook, and Campbell 2002). For example, Borden et al. (2008) investigated the effect of a seminar on students' financial knowledge and attitudes. A within-participants design for this research question may not be a good choice because exposure to the seminar (i.e., treatment) should have long-lasting benefits, and exposing students to a control condition after the seminar would be awkward. The treatment would likely still have an effect and compromise the control condition.

A pre-test/post-test design is a specific type of within-participants design such that a group is assessed before any activity (i.e., pre-test) and after any activity (i.e., post-test) on the same assessment. Pre-test/post-test designs answer the question of how students change on the assessment after implementation of the treatment. Pre-test/post-test and within-participants designs have several advantages. These designs allow for greater statistical power (Gall, Gall, and Borg 2007) and because students are compared to themselves in the different conditions, selection bias is not a problem.

However, pre-test/post-tests and within-participants designs also have several disadvantages. Although selection bias is avoided, researchers have problems because students receive multiple assessments. The first assessment may affect the second assessment, which is called a testing effect (Shadish, Cook, and Campbell 2002). To avoid the testing effect, one could use two measures for the same construct (e.g., forms A and B of a measure with different questions on each). Unfortunately, this strategy could lead to an instrumentation effect (Shadish, Cook, and Campbell 2002), which occurs if the method of measurement changes. Any increases or decreases in the assessment could be due to changes in measurement and not changes in the student. In addition, because assessments take place at different times, if anything else besides the treatment happens to the student, it may be something else that causes change and not the treatment. Not surprisingly, this problem is more likely the longer between assessments.

Minimize Disadvantages of Within-Participants Designs by Counterbalancing. Within-participants designs can have problems because one treatment may affect later treatments (i.e., carryover effect) and one assessment may affect later assessments (i.e., testing effect). Students in within-participants designs are more likely to suffer fatigue effects on later conditions (Shadish, Cook, and Campbell 2002). One strategy to minimize these problems is to counterbalance conditions. With counterbalancing, students are split into groups and exposed to different orders of conditions. For example, Herron and Tomasello (1992) investigated whether students would learn French better by deduction or guided induction. They constructed ten examples and taught five examples with each method. To counterbalance, one class received five examples with deduction and a second class received those same examples with guided induction. The researchers did the reverse with the other five examples.

Counterbalancing becomes more complicated with more conditions. Nevertheless, the purpose of allowing each condition to be placed earlier for some students and later for other students remains. Of course, counterbalancing cannot occur in pre-test/post-test designs as that would mean some students would see the post-test before the pre-test (a temporal impossibility).

Minimize Testing and Instrumentation Effects with Alternative Measures. Testing effects can be reduced by using different assessments, but different assessments cause an instrumentation effect, which is also a problem.

Researchers can use alternative measures to minimize these unwanted effects (Bartsch, Bittner, and Moreno 2008). For example, Thompson and Fisher-Thompson (2013) wanted to determine if watching a video of a study and then analyzing data from it improved students' knowledge of statistics. The researchers originally had a pre-test/post-test design. If the pre-test was the same as the post-test, any improvement could be caused by seeing the pre-test questions. If the pre-test was different than the post-test, any improvement could be caused by the post-test being easier. To minimize these problems, researchers created two versions of the test. Half the students had one version as the pre-test and the other as the post-test. The other students did the reverse. Therefore, students never received the same measure, minimizing the testing effect. Also, because both versions were taken by all students, the researcher could statistically account for any differences between the questions (i.e., avoid an instrumentation effect). Alternative measures can be used on other pre-test/post-test designs including designs with a control condition.

Add a Control Group to a Pre-Test/Post-Test Design. Between-participants designs are susceptible to selection bias. Questions arise as to whether differences between students cause any assessment differences. Pre-tests/post-tests are susceptible to confounds that occur between the initial assessment and the final assessment. A question easily raised is: what would happen with no treatment? Would the change still naturally occur? Between-participants designs without random assignment and pre-tests/post-test designs by themselves often have problems with internal validity. Internal validity can be improved by combining both designs. For example, Patrick (2010) exposed biology students to six weeks of field studies and gave them a pre-test and post-test on knowledge of science processes. Any improvement could have occurred with other forms of instruction. To minimize this problem, the researcher also had a control condition that had traditional lectures. The researcher compared the improvement in the treatment condition to improvement in the control condition. Although random assignment is important with students in separate control and treatment conditions, it is less important in this case because both groups can be compared on their pre-test assessment.

A Note about External Validity

In this chapter, I have focused on internal and construct validity. Another type of validity is external validity. External validity asks whether the sample used in the study can generalize to other groups or populations (Shaddish, Cook, and Campbell 2002). For example, would clickers used in a smaller class of thirty generalize to a larger class of two hundred? Would a class activity that improves learning with traditional students also work with nontraditional students? Would the effectiveness of social media tested on communication majors generalize to biology majors?

One facet of external validity relates to the sample. Does the sample look like other possible samples? Do students from this study look like these other students? SoTL researchers often are limited to what students they can study. Sometimes researchers can only study their own students. It is impossible in classroom studies to get a sample that will generalize to all students (Grauerholz and Main 2013). Instead, the researcher should report important demographic characteristics about students in the sample. These demographics include gender, race/ethnicity, age, year in school, and type of institution. Other demographic factors that affect the generalizability of results for a specific study (e.g., percent of first-generation college students in a study on college acculturation) should also be reported. To get this information, researchers must have archival records or ask the students these questions. I have seen many researchers writing their study suddenly remember that they should have asked these questions during data collection.

Another facet of external validity is how realistic the situation is. External validity is typically good in SoTL research because researchers often examine students in actual classes. The treatment has a high level of realism. Furthermore, if the treatment works, that provides evidence that the treatment is beneficial in some situations (Dunn 2009). In other words, knowing that the treatment has worked in one case can be useful while at the same time realizing the treatment may not work with all students.

A Note about Qualitative Studies

This chapter focuses on quantitative studies. However, qualitative studies are complementary and are just as useful. Whereas quantitative studies are empirical and specific, qualitative studies are empirical and holistic. Data are gathered in both studies, but the focus is different. Qualitative studies take a broader view of the entire situation rather than on specific measures (Thomas 2006). For example, quantitative studies would be better at answering how much of an increase in academic self-efficacy a specific treatment caused, and qualitative studies would be better at answering what are some overarching patterns in how academic self-efficacy changes during the semester. Also, qualitative methods may be better to investigate deeper levels of learning (Grauerholz and Main 2013). Researchers interested in learning more about qualitative methods should discuss their ideas with a campus expert in qualitative research.

Conclusion

The goal of this chapter is to provide suggestions to instructors turned researchers on how to create valid studies and useful SoTL research. Many of these suggestions are based on two questions. In all studies, researchers should say yes to "Am I measuring what I say I am measuring?" In addition, researchers interested in cause and effect relationships should say yes to "Can I determine causality with this design?" Remember that we as researchers should ask these questions while designing our studies, and consequently, before we collect any data, so that we know if our studies are valid.

References

Adams, C. M., and P. B. Forsyth. 2009. "Conceptualizing and Validating a Measure of Student Trust." In *Studies in School Improvement,* edited by W. Hoy and M. DiPaola, 263–280. Charlotte, NC: Information Age.

Anthis, K. 2011. "Is It the Clicker, or Is It the Question? Untangling the Effects of Student Response System Use." *Teaching of Psychology* 38: 89–93. doi:10.1177/0098628311411895.

Appleton, J. J., S. L. Christenson, D. Kim, and A. L. Reschly. 2006. "Measuring Cognitive and Psychological Engagement: Validation of the Student Engagement Instrument." *Journal of School Psychology* 44: 427–445. doi:10.1016/j.jsp.2006.04.002.

Barak, M., and Y. J. Dori. 2004. "Enhancing Undergraduate Students' Chemistry Understanding through Project-Based Learning in an IT Environment." *Science Education* 89: 117–139. doi:10.1002/sce.20027.

Bartsch, R. A. 2006, January. *The Scholarship of Teaching and Learning: How to Do and Publish Research on Teaching Activities.* Paper presented at the Society of Personality and Social Psychology Teaching Pre-Conference, Palm Springs, CA.

Bartsch, R. A., W. M. E. Bittner, and J. E. Moreno. 2008. "A Design to Improve Internal Validity of Assessments of Teaching Demonstrations." *Teaching of Psychology* 35: 357–359. doi:10.1080/00986280802373809.

Bartsch, R. A., and K. Cobern. 2003. "Effectiveness of PowerPoint Presentations in Lectures." *Computers & Education* 41: 77–86.

Borden, L. M., S. Lee, J. Serido, and D. Collins. 2008. "Changing College Students' Financial Knowledge, Attitudes, and Behavior through Seminar Participation." *Journal of Family Economic Issues* 29: 23–40. doi:10.1007/s10834-007-9087-2.

Braver, S. L., S. E. Moser, and F. Thoemmes. 2010. "Random Assignment." In *Encyclopedia of Research Design,* edited by N. Salkind, Vol. 3, 1193–1197. Washington, DC: Sage.

Dillman, D. A. 2000. *Mail and Internet Surveys: The Tailored Design Method,* 2nd ed. New York: John Wiley and Sons.

Dunn, D. S. 2009. *Research Methods for Social Psychology.* Malden, MA: Wiley-Blackwell.

Fan, S. 2010. "Independent Variable." In *Encyclopedia of Research Design,* edited by N. Salkind, Vol. 2, 591–593. Washington, DC: Sage.

Gall, M. D., J. P. Gall, and W. R. Borg. 2007. *Educational Research: An Introduction,* 8th ed. Boston, MA: Pearson.

Goldman, B. A., and D. F. Mitchell. 2007. *Directory of Unpublished Experimental Mental Measures.* Washington, DC: American Psychological Association.

Grauerholz, L., and E. Main. 2013. "Fallacies of SoTL: Rethinking How We Conduct Our Research." In *The Scholarship of Teaching and Learning in and Across the Disciplines,* edited by K. McKinney, 152–168. Bloomington: Indiana University Press.

Gurung, R. A. R., and R. E. Landrum. 2012. "Using SoTL to Improve Learning Outcomes." In *Handbook of College and University Teaching: Global Perspectives,* edited by J. Groccia, M. Alsudary, and W. Buskist, 29–44. Thousand Oaks, CA: Sage.

Hanna, D., M. Shevlin, and M. Dempster. 2008. "The Structure of the Statistics Anxiety Rating Scale: A Confirmatory Analysis Using UK Psychology Students." *Personality and Individual Differences* 45: 68–74. doi:10.1016/j.paid.2008.02.021.

Herron, C., and M. Tomasello. 1992. "Acquiring Grammatical Structures by Guided Interaction." *The French Review* 65: 708–718.

Kornell, N., and R. A. Bjork. 2008. "Learning Concepts and Categories: Is Spacing the 'Enemy of Induction?'" *Psychological Science* 19: 585–592. doi:10.1111/j.1467-9280.2008.02127.x.

Patrick, A. O. 2010. "Effects of Field Studies on Learning Outcome in Biology." *Journal of Human Ecology* 31: 171–177.

Pintrich, P. R. 2004. "A Conceptual Framework for Assessing Motivation and Self-Regulated Learning in College Students." *Educational Psychology Review* 16: 385–407.

Schwartz, B. M., and R. A. R. Gurung, eds. 2012. *Evidence-Based Teaching for Higher Education.* Washington, DC: American Psychological Association.

Shadish, W. R., T. D. Cook, and D. T. Campbell. 2002. *Experimental and Quasi-Experimental Designs for Generalized Causal Inference.* Boston: Houghton Mifflin.

Simon, D. A., and R. A. Bjork. 2001. "Metacognition in Motor Learning." *Journal of Experimental Psychology: Learning, Memory, and Cognition* 27: 907–912. doi:10.1037/0278-7393.27.4.907.

Smith, R. A. 2008. "Moving toward the Scholarship of Teaching and Learning: The Classroom Can Be a Lab, Too!" *Teaching of Psychology* 35: 262–266. doi:10.1080/00986280802418711.

Smith, R. A. 2012. "Benefits of Using SoTL in Picking and Choosing Pedagogy." In *Evidence-Based Teaching for Higher Education*, edited by B. Schwartz and R. Gurung, 7–22. Washington, DC: American Psychological Association.

Stehle, S., B. Spinath, and M. Kadmon. 2012. "Measuring Teaching Effectiveness: Correspondence between Students' Evaluations of Teaching and Different Measures of Student Learning." *Research in Higher Education* 53: 888–904. doi:10.1007/s11162-012-9260-9.

Suskie, L. 2009. *Assessing Student Learning: A Common Sense Guide*, 2nd ed. San Francisco: Jossey-Bass.

Theall, M., and K. A. Feldman. 2007. "Commentary and Update on Feldman's (1997) 'Identifying Exemplary Teachers and Teaching: Evidence from Student Ratings.'" In *The Scholarship of Teaching and Learning in Higher Education: An Evidence-Based Perspective*, edited by R. Perry and J. Smart, 130–143. Dordrecht, The Netherlands: Springer.

Thomas, D. R. 2006. "A General Inductive Approach for Analyzing Qualitative Evaluation Data." *American Journal of Evaluation* 27: 237–246. doi:10.1177/1098214005283748.

Thompson, W. B., and D. Fisher-Thompson. 2013. "Analyzing Data from Studies Depicted on Video: An Activity for Statistics and Research Courses." *Teaching of Psychology* 40: 139–142. doi:10.1177/0098628312475035.

Tomcho, T. J., and R. Foels. 2008. "Assessing Effective Teaching of Psychology: A Meta-Analytic Integration of Learning Outcomes." *Teaching of Psychology* 35: 286–296. doi:10.1080/00986280802374575.

Wesp, R., and J. Miele. 2008. "Student Opinions of the Quality of Teaching Activities Poorly Predict Pedagogical Effectiveness." *Teaching of Psychology* 35: 360–362. doi:10.1080/00986280802374617.

Wilson, J. H., S. B. Wilson, and A. M. Legg. 2012. "Building Rapport in the Classroom and Student Outcomes." In *Evidence-Based Teaching for Higher Education*, edited by B. Schwartz and R. Gurung, 23–37. Washington, DC: American Psychological Association.

Wilson-Doenges, G., and R. A. R. Gurung. 2013. "Benchmarks for Scholarly Investigations of Teaching and Learning." *Australian Journal of Psychology* 65: 63–70. doi:10.1111/ajpy.12011.

ROBERT A. BARTSCH *is an associate professor of psychology at the University of Houston-Clear Lake.*

4

This chapter suggests solutions to common practical problems in designing SoTL studies. In addition, the advantages and disadvantages of different types of designs are discussed.

Designing SoTL Studies—Part II: Practicality

Robert A. Bartsch

For a study to succeed, a design has to be valid, practical, and ethical. The previous chapter examined validity and Chapter 6 examines ethics as it relates to the Scholarship of Teaching and Learning (SoTL; see also Gurung and Schwartz 2009; Landrum and McCarthy 2012). This chapter focuses on creating practical designs. Much of SoTL is field research. The studies are done in the student's natural environment, that is, the classroom. SoTL research can be tricky because designs may not be practical due to limited numbers of students, lack of time, or inability to have more than one condition. Other designs may be practical but are not ethical. For example, I could give half my class a study guide for an exam and nothing to the other half. The study could be a practical and valid test of the effectiveness of the study guide, but ethically challenged because some students and not others may receive a benefit (see also Swenson and McCarthy 2012). Given concerns of validity, practicality, and ethics, each study has advantages and disadvantages, and researchers have to determine the advantages they need and the disadvantages they can allow.

In the next section, I discuss some common practical problems and potential solutions. Then I discuss some common designs that can be used in SoTL research. As in the previous chapter, I focus on classroom activities, which I call *treatments* (i.e., the independent variables) and the measurement of their success, which I refer to as *assessments* (i.e., the dependent variables). Also, I continue to refer to instructors doing SoTL work as researchers.

Common Practical Problems

Many times faculty are interested in SoTL research, but they do not see how it can be done. In this section, I examine some common concerns new SoTL researchers have.

New Directions for Teaching and Learning, no. 136, Winter 2013 © 2013 Wiley Periodicals, Inc.
Published online in Wiley Online Library (wileyonlinelibrary.com) • DOI: 10.1002/tl.20074

I Have to Measure Everything. Sometimes researchers get too ambitious and they measure many, many constructs. A researcher may want to determine everything about student-teacher interactions in a single study. The researcher bravely develops measures for student personality, student academic history, teaching style, students' preferred learning style, classroom characteristics, student learning, students' expected learning, students' perceived learning, and on and on. The worry is that an important construct will be missed which explains the entire area, and the strategy becomes measure everything and sort it out later. Even if every individual construct is measured well, too many constructs can cause problems with participant fatigue. Students are more likely to not think about the questions and respond with the first acceptable option and not the best answer (i.e., satisficing responses; Krosnick 1999). Additionally, too many measures make analyses much more complicated. Too often researchers create a mess of data and a headache rather than useful information. In these instances, a closer look at the literature and/or planning multiple studies can help researchers focus their study on only a few constructs.

I Do Not Have Many Students. One common limitation researchers have is that they do not have many students. Researchers may have only fifteen students in a course and may not teach the course again in the near future. A problem of testing few students is low statistical power (Wilson-Doenges and Gurung 2013). Statistical power is the ability to detect a significant finding that exists (Shadish, Cook, and Campbell 2002). In other words, low power indicates it is very likely one will not find any significant statistical effect. Researchers have only a 50 percent chance of finding a significant difference for a large effect with thirteen students in a treatment and thirteen students in a control condition (Gall, Gall, and Borg 2007). For a 70 percent chance of detecting a difference, researchers need forty total students. If it is a medium-sized effect, researchers need sixty-four students for only a 50/50 chance at finding an effect.

Power can be increased using several different methods. If one cannot increase the sample size, one can improve power by having a pre-test/post-test or other form of within-participants design (Shadish, Cook, and Campbell 2002). Researchers can detect differences more easily by seeing how students themselves change in these types of designs than other designs which separate students into treatment and control conditions.

I Only Have a Single Class. Another possible problem is the researcher only has a single class. Some designs can be used with a single group of students; however, the researcher will have greater flexibility in study design if the class can be divided. Dividing the class can cause ethical problems because only some students in the class will receive a treatment while others will be in a control condition.

LoSchiavo, Shatz, and Poling (2008) provide several ideas for how to practically split a class into groups. If the class has a web component, treatments can be given through the class course shell to only some students.

If the class splits into recitation sections, the treatment could be given during some recitation sections but not others. If neither of these is possible, the usual class time can be split such that some students arrive during the first part of class and receive the control condition and other students arrive during the second part of class and receive the treatment condition. Smith (2008) also suggests this method but goes further and states to minimize ethical concerns, students in the control condition could receive the treatment at the beginning of the next class, and the class could reunite as a whole later in the period. Researchers can also split the class and move them to separate rooms. Researchers could provide the treatment in one room and the control condition in the other (Bartsch, Case, and Meerman 2012). Finally, under some conditions, a researcher could give both the treatment and control conditions simultaneously to students in the same classroom. For example, to study the effect of question order in exams, the treatment condition may have exam questions in the order they were covered in class. The questions in the control condition may be in random order. These exams could be administered at the same time. In short, researchers have many possible options for splitting a single class into multiple groups.

Random Assignment Sounds Great, But How Can I Do It?   Random assignment of students to treatment and control conditions creates high internal validity for the study (Shadish, Cook, and Campbell 2002). Unfortunately, random assignment does not occur naturally. Having two separate classes, whether they are from the same or different semesters, is not random assignment. Except in unusual situations, students would not have had an equal chance of being in each class. Students likely self-selected which course to take based on time, day of class, availability of other classes, or whether a friend was in the class. In other words, the students in each section may differ, and these differences could be confounds. For random assignment to occur with two separate classes, students have to be randomly sorted into the two classes (e.g., students with odd-numbered student IDs are in one section, even in the other), which is uncommon in higher education. Even if random assignment occurs, classes always differ even if they are taught similarly, creating confounds (Grauerholz and Main 2013).

Random assignment can be achieved inside a single classroom more easily. In all options mentioned in the last section for splitting classes, researchers can use random assignment to assign students to the treatment and control conditions. The class can be split by choosing numbers out of a hat, flipping a coin, using a random number table, and so on (Shadish, Cook, and Campbell 2002). Even assigning students by counting "1–2–1–2..." achieves random assignment.

I Want to Detect a Subtle Effect.   Another issue to consider is whether the treatment is large enough to have an effect on the assessment. For example, using an electronic classroom response system or "clickers" one time in class or even once each week for several weeks may not cause enough of a change in students to affect the assessment. In contrast, extensive use of clickers during the semester may demonstrate a detectable effect. Larger effects have greater statistical power (Shadish, Cook, and Campbell 2002). Higher power through testing large effects can equalize other factors that decrease power such as a small sample size. For example, to have a 70 percent chance of detecting a statistically significant correlation, researchers need 23 students for a large effect, 66 students for a medium-sized effect, and 616 students for a small effect (Gall, Gall, and Borg 2007). I recommend SoTL researchers first investigate larger effects. Larger effects are easier to detect, provide instructors evidence for treatments that cause bigger changes, and provide a better foundation for future studies to explore more nuanced effects.

I Cannot Do a Valid, Ethical Study in the Classroom.   Occasionally, SoTL researchers try to create a valid, practical, and ethical field study but cannot produce a design with all three qualities. In this case, one strategy for creating a valid design is to move the study from the classroom to the laboratory, an environment where the researcher controls all the factors and does not have to worry about the ethics of teaching a class at the same time (see Bartsch and Murphy 2011, and Mayer and Johnson 2010 for examples). In the laboratory, a researcher has control to randomly assign participants who act as students (and generally are students) to conditions. Additionally, the increased control in lab studies allows researchers to more easily separate out important factors. Laboratory designs have some disadvantages. First, researchers need additional time and resources including recruiting students and finding a place to conduct the study. The second disadvantage is one of realism. Because students know the study is not for a grade, they may not try as hard as in a normal classroom situation. Lab studies complement the difficulties inherent in field studies and are a good way to begin exploration of a SoTL question.

Designs for Classroom Studies

In this section, I discuss many types of designs researchers can use in SoTL. For each design I provide a symbolic description. I have also included suggestions on when and when not to use each design. Although I present names of each design, I caution that different researchers and reference books may use different names. Of course, the name is not as important as the properties of the design. These designs are some of the more common examples. Other designs are often based on combining different parts of ones detailed here.

Simple Correlation.   Using this design (Table 4.1), researchers examine the relationships between two or more variables. For example, Baker (2010) investigated learning in online classes and correlated several variables including instructor presence, instructor immediacy, student affective learning, student motivation, and student cognitive learning. In this type of study, researchers simply measure each construct. These measurements can

Table 4.1. Simple Correlation

	Assessment 1 ↔ Assessment 2
Use If	• Have single group of students that cannot be divided • Have only one session to collect data
Do Not Use If	• Want to make statement about causality • Have low number of students
Additional Options	• Correlate many variables at same time

Table 4.2. One-Group Post-Test Only Design

	Treatment → Assessment
Use If	• Desired focus is on describing treatment and not assessment • Cannot have pre-test or control group • Have single group of students that cannot be divided
Do Not Use If	• Want to make statement about causality • Want to make comparison to another group

be collected at the same or different times. However, in these designs, it is nearly impossible to establish that one variable caused changes in another variable (Shadish, Cook, and Campbell 2002). Because all students are measured on all assessments, this design can be used when one has a single group of students.

One-Group Post-Test Only Design. In this design (Table 4.2), the researcher exposes students to a treatment and later assesses students. For example, a study may describe the novel instruction over an entire semester, and the focus of the study is about the instruction. The researchers may only collect data, such as student learning or student attitudes, to demonstrate that after taking the class, the students have a certain level of knowledge, skill, or attitudes. This conclusion of obtaining a certain level is very different from saying that a treatment caused a change or an improvement. Without a comparison group, one cannot determine if a treatment had any effect. This design is generally not recommended, and in attempting to publish the study, the design would likely be viewed as flawed.

Two-Group Post-Test Only Design. This design is the simplest of the two-group designs. In the two-group post-test only design (Table 4.3), one group receives the treatment and another does not, and then both are measured on the same assessment. For example, one set of researchers explored whether an active learning class with clicker use, student-student discussions, small group tasks, and instructor feedback on these activities would lead to more student learning and engagement than a traditional lecture with some clicker questions (Deslauriers, Schelew, and Wieman 2011). They used two separate sections of the same course and used the same exam.

Table 4.3. Two-Group Post-Test Only Design

Some Students: Treatment → Assessment
Other Students: No Treatment → Assessment

Use If	• Concerned about carryover effects • Concerned about testing and instrumentation effects • Have multiple groups • Have only one session to collect data
Do Not Use If	• Have low number of students • Groups are very different • Have different assessments for each condition
Additional Options	• Use random assignment to improve internal validity • Add post-test to assess long-term change • Add additional conditions • Use covariates to improve internal validity and power

This design has no difficulty with carryover, testing, or instrumentation effects because each student has only one treatment and is assessed one time. However, as mentioned in the last chapter, the main problem is selection bias (Shadish, Cook, and Campbell 2002). The greater the difference between the two groups, the more arguments can be made that these differences between students caused any changes on the assessment and not the treatment. If random assignment is used, then researchers can avoid questions about selection bias because random assignment should equalize groups on all characteristics except for the treatment (Shadish, Cook, and Campbell 2002). A second problem with the design has to do with the relatively low statistical power of a comparison between groups (Shadish, Cook, and Campbell 2002). If class sizes are small, significant differences are difficult to detect.

Researchers may decide to have more than one treatment and one control condition. For example, Chang, Sung, and Chen (2001) studied the effects of concept mapping on learning. They had three conditions. Students either constructed a concept map by themselves, using a computer without hints, or using a computer with hints. In this case, the researchers not only can test the difference between not using and using a computer, but also how to best use the computer. Also, researchers may have more than two conditions because the treatment occurs in a range. As an example, researchers investigated how instructor self-disclosure on Facebook affected students' impression of the class instructor (Mazer, Murphy, and Simonds 2007). The researchers created high, medium, and low self-disclosure levels for the instructor. Using three levels allowed researchers to see the effect at the extremes and a more moderate value. Of course, studies with more than two conditions need more students. Researchers should have a minimum of ten students in each condition (Wilson-Doenges and Gurung 2013).

One-Group Pre-Test/Post-Test Design. With this design (Table 4.4), the researcher measures students before the treatment and then after

Table 4.4. One-Group Pre-Test/Post-Test Design

Assessment → Treatment → Assessment

Use If	• Have low number of students • Have single group of students that cannot be divided • Cannot have control condition
Do Not Use If	• Items other than treatment occur between assessments • First assessment, by itself, affects second assessment • Students are likely to change between assessments with no treatment
Additional Options	• Add post-test to assess long-term change • Use alternative measures to minimize testing and instrumentation effects

Table 4.5. Two-Group Pre-Test/Post-Test Design

Some Students: Assessment → Treatment → Assessment
Other Students: Assessment → No Treatment → Assessment

Use If	• Have multiple groups
Do Not Use If	• Have single group of students that cannot be divided
Additional Options	• Use random assignment to improve internal validity • Add post-test to assess long-term change • Use alternative measures to minimize testing and instrumentation effects • Add additional conditions • Use covariates to improve internal validity and power

the treatment to determine any changes. For example, Bridges et al. (1998) wanted students to learn more quantitative reasoning in a non-method sociology course. After adding material to their class, they measured students at the beginning and end of the semester on quantitative reasoning.

Because it has a single group and compares students to themselves, the design is very useful with low numbers of students. This design has some disadvantages. Students or the environment may change naturally between the two assessments. This design cannot separate any natural changes from changes caused by the treatment. Additionally, the first assessment may affect the response on the second assessment (i.e., testing effect; Shadish, Cook, and Campbell 2002), especially if the questions are the same and the assessments are close together. Unfortunately, having different questions at the pre- and post-tests can lead to an instrumentation effect (Shadish, Cook, and Campbell 2002). These issues can be minimized using alternative measures (Bartsch, Bittner, and Moreno 2008).

Two-Group Pre-Test/Post-Test Design. This design (Table 4.5) has a treatment and control condition. Both groups are assessed before and after the treatment. As an example, Williams (2005) examined whether

Table 4.6. Within-Participants Design

Treatment 1 → Assessment → Treatment 2 → Assessment → [Continues]	
Use If	• Have low number of students
	• Have single group of students that cannot be divided
Do Not Use If	• Early treatments affect later treatments
	• Early assessments affect later assessments
Additional Options	• Add additional treatments
	• Counterbalance conditions to improve internal validity
	• Include pre-test to assess students before any treatment

participation in study abroad programs increased students' intercultural communication skills. Williams measured at the beginning and end of the semester students who participated and did not participate in a study abroad program.

With the pre-test, equalizing student differences between conditions becomes less important because the researcher has a baseline on each person for comparison. Of course, whenever possible researchers should randomly assign students to the treatment and control conditions.

The two-group pre-test/post-test design does not have major disadvantages, but because the design has multiple assessments, researchers should check on any testing and/or instrumentation effects. These can be minimized with alternative measures (Bartsch, Bittner, and Moreno 2008). Given the nature of field research and the difficulty of having random assignment, this design is often a good balance between validity and practicality.

Within-Participants Design. In this design (Table 4.6), each student is in each condition, and each student is assessed after each condition. Sometimes the study has a treatment and a control condition, or may have two similar treatment conditions. The study can also have more than two conditions. For example, one study examined the effectiveness of Power-Point presentations (Bartsch and Cobern 2003). In this study, researchers rotated between three conditions: overhead transparencies, plain Power-Point slides, and PowerPoint slides with pictures, graphs, transitions, and sound effects. Conditions rotated each week, and each week researchers quizzed the students.

The strength of within-participants designs is that researchers do not need as many students in their studies. Counterbalancing conditions is recommended to improve internal validity. With counterbalancing, different students take treatments in different orders to minimize carryover effects (Dunn 2009). Of course, to counterbalance, students have to be split into different groups.

Crossover Design. In this design (Table 4.7; Shadish, Cook, and Campbell 2002), students are split into two groups. One group receives the treatment, both groups are assessed, then the other group receives the treatment, and both groups are assessed again. The crossover design is a

Table 4.7. Crossover Design

Some Students: Treatment → Assessment → No Treatment → Assessment
Other Students: No Treatment → Assessment → Treatment → Assessment

Use If	• Have low number of students • Have multiple groups
Do Not Use If	• First assessment, by itself, affects second assessment • Have single group of students that cannot be divided
Additional Options	• Include pre-test to assess students before any treatment • Add post-test to examine long-term change • Use random assignment to improve internal validity • Use alternative measures to minimize testing and instrumentation effects

Table 4.8. Interrupted Time-Series Design

Multiple Assessments → Treatment → Multiple Assessments

Use If	• Have low number of students • Have single group of students that cannot be divided • Want to determine long-term effects
Do Not Use If	• Have only one session to collect data • Early assessments affect later assessments
Additional Options	• Add control condition to improve internal validity • Add additional treatment condition, with treatment at different time to improve internal validity

counterbalanced within-participants design with two conditions. For example, Ocker and Yaverbaum (1999) wanted to determine any differences in performance and preference on a case study between face-to-face groups and groups using asynchronous computer collaboration. They used two case studies. Some student groups did the first case study face-to-face and the second asynchronously on the computer. Other student groups did the first case study on the computer and the second face-to-face.

In crossover designs, researchers need to make sure the first assessment does not by itself cause changes on the second assessment. This potential problem can be minimized by using related assessments or by alternative measures. In Ocker and Yaverbaum's research it would have been meaningless to assess the same case study under both conditions, and consequently they used two separate cases.

Interrupted Time-Series Design.   In this design (Table 4.8; Shadish, Cook, and Campbell 2002), multiple pre-tests occur before and multiple post-tests occur after the treatment. For example, suppose researchers want to assess students' self-efficacy across time. They measure self-efficacy every two weeks. Halfway through the semester, the researchers stage an intervention to change self-efficacy. This time-series design can determine the stability of scores before treatment (i.e., the intervention) and can examine the effect of the treatment over a longer period of time. This design minimizes the problem with a one sample pre-test/post-test design of students naturally changing.

Researchers can also include a control condition. The same assessments occur at the same time but students in the control condition do not receive the treatment. The control condition strengthens the internal validity of the study. Similarly, researchers could also have another condition but that condition receives the treatment at a different time. In this design, we expect similar changes to occur for both groups after they receive the treatment condition. Because treatments occur at different times, the predicted change should occur at different times. This design rules out many possible confounds enhancing the internal validity of the study. These designs work well without random assignment. Of course, another group of students needs to be available.

More Complex Designs

As SoTL research becomes more sophisticated, we will begin to move away from simpler research questions such as whether this treatment causes a change in assessment. Rather researchers will build on the simple statement to more complex questions. This final section looks at some of these designs.

Use Multiple Treatments to Investigate Interactions. So far in the chapter, I discussed designs with only one treatment or independent variable. However, many research designs have more than one treatment. For example, Chesbro (2003) manipulated both nonverbal immediacy of an instructor and instructor clarity to determine how students respond to both student learning and student affect. Nonverbal immediacy and clarity are two separate treatments. Each one may have an effect and an interaction may occur between the two treatments. Think of these interactions like medical drug interactions. Sometimes combining different drugs causes very different results than just adding their individual effects. Only by testing multiple treatments at once can researchers investigate how the treatments interact with each other.

Use Moderators to Determine When Treatment Has Effect. Instead of asking whether a treatment works, researchers may ask under what conditions or when does the treatment change the assessment. The moderator alters the effect of the treatment on the assessment (Baron and Kenny 1986). Cole, Field, and Harris (2004) investigated whether psychological hardiness moderated the effect of learning motivation on reactions to classroom experience. In other words, they asked whether students who are low on psychological hardiness have a different motivation-experience relationship than students high on psychological hardiness. In another example, I may be interested in whether clickers work better on first-generation college students or non-first-generation college students. In this case, whether a student is first-generation is the moderating variable, and the relationship between clickers and student success may differ between first-generation and non-first-generation students. These questions allow researchers to probe under what conditions these effects exist.

A moderating variable is statistically equivalent to a second treatment described in the previous section. The difference is the label and context. Oftentimes using multiple treatments, the researcher is interested in all treatments individually and their interaction. With moderators, researchers are more interested in the effect the treatment has on the assessment and how the moderating variable influences that effect. Typically, researchers do not care about the effect of the moderator by itself on the assessment.

Use Mediators to Investigate How Treatment Has Effect.   Another more complex design is a mediational analysis. The main question asked in this type of analysis is how the treatment causes change in the assessment. Mediators delve into the process of what happens with students and "account for the relation" between the treatment and assessment (Baron and Kenny 1986, 1176). For example, Elliot, McGregor, and Gable (1999) wanted to investigate more deeply the relationship between motivational goals and exam scores. They found persistence of effort mediated the relationship between performance approach goals and exam scores, and disorganization mediated the relationship between performance avoidance goals and exam scores. Therefore, according to their analysis, a performance approach goal leads to more persistence which then leads to higher exam scores and a performance avoidance goal leads to more disorganization which leads to lower exam scores. These mediators suggest the mechanism behind the overall motivational goal-exam score relationship.

Conclusion

SoTL research can be difficult given its many practical limitations. Table 4.9 summarizes the different types of designs presented and which designs should be used with small samples or single classes. The table also describes which designs allow researchers to complete the study in a single session, whether the design is set to detect long-term effects, and if the design supports causal claims. The suggestions provided in the table and this chapter hopefully will help future researchers create practical designs to test their research questions.

Each design has advantages and disadvantages. Although there may be better and worse ways to design and conduct a study, there will never be *one* clear right way. There is no single ideal study that eliminates all potential problems and all alternative hypotheses. There is no one study that answers

Table 4.9. Summary of When and When Not to Use Designs

Design	Use with Small Samples	Use with Single Class	Can Complete in One Session	Can Determine Long-term Effects	Can Determine Causal Relationships	Main Weaknesses
Simple correlation	No	Yes	Yes	No	No	Cannot determine causality
One-group post-test only	Yes	Yes	Yes	No	No	Cannot make comparisons; cannot determine causality
Two-group post-test only	No	If class can be divided	Yes	If add long-term post-test	Yes with random assignment; typically no without	Selection bias
One-group pre-test/post-test	Yes	Yes	If pre- and post-test in same session	If add long-term post-test	Depends on context	Testing and instrumentation effects; confounds between assessments
Two-group pre-test/post-test	Maybe	If class can be divided	If pre- and post-test in same session	If add long-term post-test	Typically yes, better with random assignment	Various minor issues depending on context
Within participants	Yes	Yes	If all treatments and assessments in same session	No	Typically yes if counterbalanced	Carryover, testing, and instrumentation effects
Crossover	Yes	If class can be divided	If both treatments and assessments in same session	If add long-term post-test	Typically yes	Testing and instrumentation effects
Interrupted time series	Yes	Yes	No	Yes	Typically yes	Testing and instrumentation effects

all questions. The strength of science, including SoTL research, does not lie in one individual study, but rather that a large number of studies from a large number of researchers who together push the boundaries of what we know.

References

Baker, C. 2010. "The Impact of Instructor Immediacy and Presence for Online Student Affective Learning, Cognition, and Motivation." *Journal of Educators Online* 7 (1): 1–30.

Baron, R. M., and D. A. Kenny. 1986. "The Moderator–Mediator Variable Distinction in Social Psychological Research: Conceptual, Strategic, and Statistical Considerations." *Journal of Personality and Social Psychology* 51: 1173–1182. doi:10.1037/0022-3514.51.6.1173.

Bartsch, R. A., W. M. E. Bittner, and J. E. Moreno. 2008. "A Design to Improve Internal Validity of Assessments of Teaching Demonstrations." *Teaching of Psychology* 35: 357–359. doi:10.1080/00986280802373809.

Bartsch, R. A., K. A. Case, and H. Meerman. 2012. "Increasing Academic Self-Efficacy in Statistics with a Live Vicarious Experience Presentation." *Teaching of Psychology* 39: 133–136. doi:10.1177/0098628312437699.

Bartsch, R. A., and K. Cobern. 2003. "Effectiveness of PowerPoint Presentations in Lectures." *Computers and Education* 41: 77–86.

Bartsch, R. A., and W. Murphy. 2011. "Examining the Effects of an Electronic Classroom Response System on Student Engagement and Performance." *Journal of Educational Computing Research* 44 (1): 25–33. doi:10.2190/EC.44.1.b.

Bridges, G. S., G. M. Gillmore, J. L. Pershing, and K. A. Bates. 1998. "Teaching Quantitative Research Methods: A Quasi-Experimental Analysis." *Teaching Sociology* 26: 14–28.

Chang, K. E., Y. T. Sung, and S. F. Chen. 2001. "Learning through Computer-Based Concept Mapping with Scaffolding Aid." *Journal of Computer Assisted Learning* 17: 21–33.

Chesbro, J. L. 2003. "Effects of Teacher Clarity and Nonverbal Immediacy on Student Learning, Receiver Apprehension, and Affect." *Communication Education* 52: 135–147.

Cole, M. S., H. S. Field, and S. G. Harris. 2004. "Student Learning Motivation and Psychological Hardiness: Interactive Effects on Students' Reactions to a Management Class." *Academy of Management Learning and Education* 3: 64–85.

Deslauriers, L., E. Schelew, and C. Wieman. 2011. "Improved Learning in a Large-Enrollment Physics Class." *Science* 332: 862–864. doi:10.1126/science.1201783.

Dunn, D. S. 2009. *Research Methods for Social Psychology*. Malden, MA: Wiley-Blackwell.

Elliot, A. J., H. A. McGregor, and S. Gable. 1999. "Achievement Goals, Study Strategies, and Exam Performance: A Mediational Analysis." *Journal of Educational Psychology* 91: 549–563.

Gall, M. D., J. P. Gall, and W. R. Borg. 2007. *Educational Research: An Introduction*, 8th ed. Boston: Pearson.

Grauerholz, L., and E. Main. 2013. "Fallacies of SoTL: Rethinking How We Conduct Our Research." In *The Scholarship of Teaching and Learning in and across the Disciplines*, edited by K. McKinney, 152–168. Bloomington: Indiana University Press.

Gurung, R. A. R., and B. M. Schwartz. 2009. *Optimizing Teaching and Learning: Practicing Pedagogical Approach*. Chichester, West Sussex, UK: Wiley-Blackwell.

Krosnick, J. A. 1999. "Survey Research." *Annual Review of Psychology* 50: 537–567.

Landrum, R. E., and M. A. McCarthy. 2012. *Teaching Ethically: Challenges and Opportunities.* Washington, DC: American Psychological Association.

LoSchiavo, F. M., M. A. Shatz, and M. A. Poling. 2008. "Strengthening the Scholarship of Teaching and Learning via Experimentation." *Teaching of Psychology* 35: 301–304. doi:10.1080/00986280802377164.

Mayer, R. E., and C. I. Johnson. 2010. "Adding Instructional Features that Promote Learning in a Game-Like Environment." *Journal of Educational Computing Research* 42: 241–265. doi:10.2190/EC.42.3.a.

Mazer, J. P., R. E. Murphy, and C. J. Simonds. 2007. "I'll See You on 'Facebook': The Effects of Computer-Mediated Teacher Self-Disclosure on Student Motivation, Affective Learning, and Classroom Climate." *Communication Education* 56 (1): 1–17. doi:10.1080/03634520601009710.

Ocker, R. J., and G. J. Yaverbaum. 1999. "Asynchronous Computer-Mediated Communication versus Face-to-Face Collaboration: Results on Student Learning, Quality and Satisfaction." *Group Decision and Negotiation* 8: 427–440.

Shadish, W. R., T. D. Cook, and D. T. Campbell. 2002. *Experimental and Quasi-Experimental Designs for Generalized Causal Inference.* Boston: Houghton Mifflin.

Smith, R. A. 2008. "Moving toward the Scholarship of Teaching and Learning: The Classroom Can Be a Lab, Too!" *Teaching of Psychology* 35: 262–266. doi:10.1080/00986280802418711.

Swenson, E. V., and M. A. McCarthy. 2012. "Ethically Conducting the Scholarship of Teaching and Learning Research." In *Teaching Ethically: Challenges and Opportunities,* edited by R. Landrum and M. McCarthy, 21–29. Washington, DC: American Psychological Association.

Williams, T. R. 2005. "The Impact of Study Abroad on Students' Intercultural Communication Skills: Adaptability and Sensitivity." *Journal of Studies in International Education* 9: 356–371. doi:10.1177/1028315305277681.

Wilson-Doenges, G., and R. A. R. Gurung. 2013. "Benchmarks for Scholarly Investigations of Teaching and Learning." *Australian Journal of Psychology* 65: 63–70. doi:10.1111/ajpy.12011.

ROBERT A. BARTSCH *is an associate professor of psychology at the University of Houston-Clear Lake.*

5

This chapter will provide potential models for analyzing learning data through a discussion of screening data and then analyzing that data using appropriate statistical techniques.

Statistical Models for Analyzing Learning Data

Georjeanna Wilson-Doenges

Oftentimes we find ourselves with a plethora of data on teaching and learning but lack the direction needed to find the best way to analyze these data. We collect and often grade many different assessments over the course of a semester, offering numerous and diverse outcomes. If we want to truly understand, utilize, and disseminate what we learn from these assessments, analyzing the data using an appropriate and rigorous method will help us do just that. Knowing that what we do in the classroom is having an impact on students' learning above what might happen just by chance alone is an important motivator for using statistical analyses (Gurung and Schwartz 2009). Selecting the optimal analysis is often the most difficult part in the research process. The previous chapters outlined some design models to measure student success. The current chapter will build on that foundation, providing potential models for analyzing the learning data that have been collected. It should be said at the outset of this chapter that statistical analysis is only as good as the data collected. Using appropriate and rigorous data collection methods provides results with the most integrity (Wilson-Doenges and Gurung 2013).

Why Do We Need Statistical Analyses Anyway?

For many disciplines, the question of "analyzing" does not even come up. Social science methodology involves significance testing. It is not enough to just observe change in student learning, but it is important to ask if that change was statistically significant. Assessing change is one type of pedagogical endeavor that necessitates the quantitative method regardless of discipline. If you want to know if students improved after a change you made (e.g., a new assignment, an innovative presentation, group work, or

NEW DIRECTIONS FOR TEACHING AND LEARNING, no. 136, Winter 2013 © 2013 Wiley Periodicals, Inc.
Published online in Wiley Online Library (wileyonlinelibrary.com) • DOI: 10.1002/tl.20075

flipping your class), you need to know if that change would have happened by chance or if any other factors could account for it (Gurung 2013). When social scientists ask if the change is statistically significant, they really want to ensure that the change is due to what was done and not just by chance. Stated in this way, it seems hard to not care about statistical significance. If you have worked hard to change your instruction and improve student learning, it is important to know whether that change would have happened by chance and without your intervention in the first place. Before one spends more time and energy on changing instruction or even trying to get others to also change instruction based on the changes you have seen, you should be sure that your changes are not random. Statistical testing does this for you.

Getting Ready to Analyze Data: Data Cleaning and Screening

Statistical analysis is most easily accomplished by taking advantage of a computer software package licensed for use through your institution. Programs like Excel, SPSS, and SAS make the process of analysis easier to accomplish. First, you will need to get your data into a software package by hand-entering or importing the data you have collected (see Gurung and Schwartz 2009 for information about entering data into SPSS). Before analysis begins, it is always a good idea to clean and screen your data. Data entry is often a cumbersome and boring task that leads to errors, so identifying data that have been entered in error or identifying data that are correct, but potentially unexpected, is an important first step in your data analysis. "Eyeballing" the information you entered, that is, looking over the entered exam or quiz scores, for instance, in a spreadsheet format is one way to look for unusual values, but of course, this is neither efficient nor extremely accurate. A better way to accomplish this task is to use the capacities of the computer program to run frequency tables, graphs, and basic descriptive statistics on all your variables. Looking for minimum or maximum values that are outside of the range of possible values is one way to find incorrect data. For example, if I used a scale of 1 (*strongly disagree*) to 5 (*strongly agree*) but found in my frequency table a minimum value of 0 or a maximum value of 55, then I would know to go back and correct those two entries after checking the raw data.

After obvious problems have been cleaned, data screening can begin. Data screening also uses frequency tables and descriptive statistics, but more importantly involves diagnostic tests. Data screening performs several important functions, including bringing to your attention issues of violations of assumptions, missing data, and variability.

Data screening can ensure that your data (e.g., exam scores) meet the assumptions of the statistical tests you plan to use. All statistical tests have standards that the data must meet in order to use a particular test. For example, *t*-tests and analysis of variance (ANOVA) tests have the assumption of normality. One way to check whether your data are likely to meet this assumption is by using data screening normality tests, such as tests of skewness and kurtosis or the Kolmogorov–Smirnov (K–S) statistic. Violations of the normality assumption can be seen by values of skewness and kurtosis that are far from zero (where zero represents normally distributed data) or a significant K–S statistic (*significance* less than .05; Field 2013). Most statistical tests are robust to moderate violations of these assumptions (e.g., ANOVA tests are robust to moderate violations of normality such as a K–S statistic p value close to, but not less than, .05; Elliot and Woodward 2007), especially when your sample size is large. However, smaller sample sizes may be a reason to pay more attention to data screening since small sample sizes are less robust to violations of assumptions (Field 2013). If your sample size is small (e.g., a class size of 20) and your initial data screening shows that your dependent variable of exam scores is very skewed, you may consider addressing skew with a data transformation before further analyses (see Field 2013 for information about data transformation).

Another important function of data screening is highlighting problems with missing data. Randomly scattered missing data are inevitable, like a student being absent for class during a quiz. But missing data that follow a pattern are more cause for concern. Tabachnick and Fidell (2012) give the qualifier that if 5 percent or less of your data are missing randomly without an apparent pattern, missing values would not be a serious issue. However, if this is not the case, identifying patterns of missing data and then addressing that concern are important. An example might be if you are measuring self-reported grade point average (GPA) and attitudes toward the class. If several students refuse to answer the self-reported GPA question, it is likely that refusal to answer that question is related to attitudes toward the class and would therefore not be random. Common solutions to missing data include deletion of any case with missing data (used mostly when missing data are random and few), estimation of missing data using the mean or regression, and expectation maximization (Tabachnick and Fidell 2012). The first solution of deletion of cases with any missing data can be misleading if missing data follow a pattern. For example, if students who miss quizzes are consistently the worst performers in the class, then not including any of their scores in your analyses because of missing data on some quizzes may be misleading to your overall findings. Let us use a scenario where you are looking at the impact of an active-learning activity on quiz scores between quiz 4 and quiz 5 in your class. You discover through data screening that students who have the lowest overall grade in the class were also the most likely to have missing data on a quiz. In your analysis of differences between quiz 4 and quiz 5, deleting students with missing data from the analysis may mask improvements between quiz 4 and quiz 5 if these worst performers are removed from the analysis because they had missing data on quiz 4. If the worst performers are removed from the analysis, then the impact of the activity is only being tested on the better performers in the class. A better approach may be to substitute the mean of quiz 1 through quiz 3 for a missing score on quiz 4 so that a comparison can be made with quiz 5 to test the hypothesis using the full sample including those who missed quiz 4. By using estimation of quiz scores for missing data, you have utilized the full sample to make the best comparisons (see Tabachnick and Fidell 2012 for information about estimation of missing values).

Data screening can also draw your attention to variables with little variability or very low frequencies for some answer categories. For example, it is difficult to find significant differences between exams if those exam scores have little variability and low frequency of poor scores. If all students receive grades near 90 percent on the first exam, then detecting changes between the first exam and the final exam may be difficult. Commonly referred to as the ceiling effect, high scores are hard to improve in a significant way. So even though the teaching improvement may actually have an impact on student learning, the exams are not able to detect those improvements because nearly everyone scored so well. Unfortunately, there is no "cure" for the ceiling effect once it happens, although writing exams that test a fuller spectrum of student understanding could help increase variability.

Creating Summative Variables

At the start of analysis is also a time to create new variables that may be summative. Often, the creation of a scale or inventory score will require adding scores on multiple items to measure a variable, and reverse scoring of some items may be needed as well. For instance, in a recent study of ideal teacher behaviors, Komarraju (2013) used several summative scales including the Teacher Behaviors Checklist (TBC; Keeley, Smith, and Buskist 2006), which is a composite of twenty-eight responses summed. After creating a composite score, it is crucial to check and report the internal consistency or reliability of that created scale. The most common method is to calculate Cronbach's alpha, a statistic that measures the average inter-correlation between every item in a composite score (for interpretation see Field 2013). A Cronbach's alpha of greater than .7 is typically considered to represent good reliability (Field 2013). Higher alpha levels indicate more cohesiveness among items. In Komarraju's study, the TBC "caring" subscale of eleven items had an alpha of .78, and the "professional" subscale of thirteen items had an alpha of .82, showing good reliability (Komarraju 2013).

Understanding Some Basics of Statistical Analysis

Now that your data have been cleaned, screened, and prepared, analysis can begin. The basic structure of statistical analysis is hypothesis testing. Hypothesis testing sets up two hypotheses: null and alternative. The null hypothesis illustrates the notion that there is not a difference between groups, no association between variables, or no effect; the alternative hypothesis offers the idea that the null hypothesis is false, and any observed differences, associations, or effects are statistically significant. When comparing groups, these hypotheses can be tested either one- or two-tailed, but one-tailed hypotheses should only be used when there is a strong a priori rationale for doing so (e.g., you have good reason to believe that you know which group will be higher than the other). Decisions are made based on the null hypothesis, in that when a finding is significant, the null hypothesis is rejected; when a finding is not significant, we fail to reject the null hypothesis. For example, if the correlation between time spent studying and students' exam scores is significant, then we would reject the null hypothesis. In other words, we reject the idea that no relationship exists.

Type I and Type II Errors and Power

When a researcher makes a decision regarding the null hypothesis (either reject or fail to reject), this decision is reached with the knowledge that there always is a chance the decision is incorrect. Two types of errors can occur: Type I and Type II errors. Type I error is determining that there is a significant finding, when in reality no meaningful effect exists (e.g., saying there is a significant correlation between time spent studying and exam scores when, in the population of students, there really is no such relationship). The chance (or probability) of making this kind of error is referred to as the level of significance or the alpha (α) level. In the social and behavioral sciences, we most commonly set acceptable probability of Type I error at $\alpha = .05$, meaning that we will accidentally say we found an effect when no effect exists 5 percent of the time. Type II error refers to the failure to reject a false null hypothesis, or failure to detect a significant result when one existed (e.g., finding that there is not a significant relationship between time spent studying and exam scores when, in the population of students, a meaningful relationship existed). Commonly regarded acceptable probability of Type II error is .20 or 20 percent of the time (Field 2013).

Related to Type II error is the power of the statistical test to detect significant findings. Determining acceptable power in your research is based on the effect size (how big of an effect you are expecting), sample size, and the α level. Running a power analysis using a computer application or the tables provided in Cohen (1988) will help you determine how big of a sample size you will need to gain acceptable power (and the resulting probability of Type II error) for your analyses. Typically, we would like power to be .80, which results in probability of Type II error of .20. Of course, power is best addressed in the planning stage of your research so that large enough sample sizes are collected to gain acceptable power (Field 2013). For instance, if testing the effects of online tutorials on increased student understanding of the course content in one section of your class compared to a section of your class with no tutorials, if you are expecting a moderate effect size and you set $\alpha = .05$ and power $= .80$, then an acceptable sample size would be approximately thirty-five students in each section.

Effect Size

When using hypothesis testing to determine statistical significance, it is important to also report a measure of practical significance as well. Understanding the size of a significant effect puts the findings into a real-world context. Effect sizes (typically measured using Cohen's d, Pearson correlation coefficient r, or partial eta squared η_p^2) are important to note because they give us an idea of the magnitude of the statistically significant finding in standardized form that can be compared more generally (Field 2013). According to Cohen (1988), a small effect size would be less than .20, medium is in the vicinity of .50, and large would be more than .80.

Summary of Main Strategies for Analyzing Learning Data

Determining the appropriate statistical analysis relies on identifying both the type of variables (nominal, ordinal, interval, and ratio) and the number of variables used to answer a particular research question. In what follows, I will suggest some common analytic techniques to answer questions based on the design strategies put forth in the previous chapters. Of course, there are a multitude of different research scenarios for which special analyses would be appropriate, but this list will cover the main analyses you would use.

One-Group, Post-Test Only.   It is clear that the one-group, post-test design is not recommended (see Chapter 4). The analytic strategy makes the flaws in this design evident in that there are no comparisons to make. So all you can do is use descriptive statistics to describe data without being able to say whether the activity or method influenced those data.

One-Group Pre-Test, Post-Test Design (Repeated-Measures Design).   A repeated-measures design is used to assess whether learning was potentially influenced by the teaching innovation by comparing a pre-test (baseline) score to a post-test (after CLASS) score. For this design, a repeated-measures or paired-samples t-test could be used to assess whether the mean at post-test is significantly different than the mean at pre-test, considering that the same students have taken both tests. This model is limited to just two measurements. For example, in a study of a weeklong training program for teaching assistants, a paired-samples t-test showed a significant increase in the personal efficacy of teaching assistants from pre-test to post-test, $t(81) = 7.40$, $p < .001$, $d = .64$ (Komarraju 2006). This finding shows a statistically significant difference between pre-test and post-test scores with a moderate effect size.

Repeated-Measures Design.   A repeated-measures ANOVA would be appropriate to determine if a teaching innovation has a significant effect on learning when learning is assessed multiple times before and/or after the teaching innovation is implemented. This analysis would be accomplished in a two-step approach, where an F-test first is used to test for overall significant differences among the means in the repeated-measures design. Second, post-hoc tests would be used to determine where significant differences actually occur. If the teaching innovation worked, significant differences should appear between assessments pre-teaching innovation and post-teaching innovation. For example, in a study of a graduate preparation program, a group of students completed a Grad Prep Quiz three times (Neimeyer et al. 2004). These students participated in a graduate preparation program between Time 2 and Time 3. A repeated-measures ANOVA showed a significant difference in Grad Prep Quiz score across the three times, $F(2, 24) = 35.33$, $p < .0001$. Using post-hoc tests, the researchers found no significant difference between Time 1 and Time 2 Grad Prep Quiz scores, but they found a significant difference between Time 3 and both Time 1 and Time 2 scores on the Grad Prep Quiz (Neimeyer et al. 2004). These findings illustrate that significant gains were made in Grad Prep Quiz score after students participated in the graduate preparation program.

Between-Groups Design.   When comparing groups on the same dependent variable, commonly with one group that has received the CLASS and the others that have not, the independent-samples t-test and ANOVA are the most appropriate statistical approaches. A common flaw in this design is evident in the lack of pre-test (see Chapter 4 for details). In a simple form, a one-way, between-groups ANOVA would test differences in the mean dependent variable between the levels of the independent variable (receiving the CLASS or not). As with other tests, reporting the effect size (measured using Cohen's d or η_p^2) is important with a significant effect. For example, in a study of exam performance between students who used three different classroom-response methods, Elicker and McConnell (2011) found no significant exam score differences between students who used technology-based network systems, hand-held flash cards, or hand raising. However, they did find significant differences in student attitudes toward the three response methods, $F(2, 205) = 5.34$, $p = .005$, $\eta_p^2 = .050$, where students using the technology-based response method reported significantly higher satisfaction than those using flash cards but not as compared to those using hand raising, nor between flash cards and hand raising (Elicker and McConnell 2011).

There are more complex variations to this simple model, such as a factorial ANOVA, which would test the combined effect of two factors such as the independent variable (teaching innovation) and time that the class meets (8:00 versus 2:00). The statistical model would include main effects and an interaction measuring the combined influence of the factors on an outcome of interest (e.g., final grades). For example, in a study of

Student Response Systems (SRS) and level of the course (200 level versus 500 level), an ANOVA revealed significant main effects for SRS use and level of the course on student engagement and student absences. In addition, SRS and level of the course interacted to influence absences where the 500-level course with SRS had the significantly lowest number of absences (Fortner-Wood et al. 2013).

Another variation to test between-groups differences would be analysis of covariance (ANCOVA). ANCOVA is used when an additional variable is statistically controlled or removed from the analysis. Removing such a covariate generally provides a clearer effect of the main factor(s) of interest, if a significant effect exists. ANCOVA is appropriate when considering an additional factor intrinsic to the participant (e.g., GPA or ACT score). In order for ANCOVA to be appropriate, the covariate must be quantitative and significantly correlated with the dependent variable (Berkman and Reise 2012). In the SRS study described in the previous paragraph, cumulative grade point average (GPA) was used as a covariate in an ANCOVA model and showed that the original ANOVA results persisted when GPA was controlled in the ANCOVA analysis (Fortner-Wood et al. 2013). Including GPA in this model helps the researchers see the effect of SRS on absences after taking into account the impact of GPA on absences. This gives the researchers a clearer picture of the impact of the SRS variable.

Mixed-ANOVA Design. Another analysis often used in SoTL research is a mixed-ANOVA design, which involves both between-groups and repeated-measures factors. In SoTL research, the repeated-measures component is often a pre-test and post-test assessment (e.g., first and final exams), and the between-groups component might include one group exposed to a new teaching technique and a control group not exposed. One way to accomplish a mixed-ANOVA design would be to create change scores by calculating a new variable: the difference between the post-test and pre-test scores. Using this newly created change score, an independent-samples t-test or ANOVA can be used to test between-groups differences as discussed in the previous section. In other words, is the change in demonstration of learning significantly different between the group exposed to the CLASS and the control group? Following from the logic of the previous section, factorial ANOVA or ANCOVA could also be used as needed.

A second way to test this type of design would be to use a mixed between-within design. This is appropriate because the CLASS variable is a between-groups factor, and the multiple measures of the dependent variable serve as the within factor (Tabachnick and Fidell 2012). Tests would include main effects as well as the potential for an interaction between the two factors. For example, in a mixed-design study of student grade expectations over the years in school between technical, two-year, and four-year institutions, McCann et al. (2013) found significance over the years in school as well as between types of institutions. Specifically, one of their findings was that expected sophomore grades were significantly higher than expected first-year grades (repeated-measures), and expected grades at the four-year institutions were significantly lower than at the two-year institutions (between-groups; McCann et al. 2013).

Correlational Designs. Some SoTL research is not experimental or quasi-experimental; we are not manipulating a variable in the teaching-learning environment but rather looking at associations between variables. In such instances, correlation is a way to test the statistical significance of an association between two quantitative variables. The larger the Pearson correlation coefficient r value, the stronger the association (with a maximum of ± 1.00). For example, in a study testing the reliability and validity of a rubric-type assessment of APA-style writing, Greenberg (2012) correlated her scoring instrument with cumulative GPA and found them to be significantly related. This research is a great example of the type of scenario when correlation is useful in testing associations rather than experimental manipulations.

In summary, learning data are varied, and using an appropriate analytic strategy increases your chances of publishing your study and sharing your findings with a wider audience. This chapter has provided potential models for doing just that: analyzing learning data. Through a discussion of screening data and then analyzing that data using appropriate statistical techniques, this chapter has given you a basic approach to tackling analysis of learning data. Being able to assess the impact of what we do in our classrooms on students' learning in rigorous ways allows us to share what we know to ultimately improve teaching and learning.

References

Berkman, E. T., and S. P. Reise. 2012. *A Conceptual Guide to Statistics Using SPSS*. Los Angeles: Sage.

Cohen, J. 1988. *Statistical Power Analysis for the Behavioral Sciences*. Hillsdale, NJ: Lawrence Erlbaum Associates.

Elicker, J. D., and N. L. McConnell. 2011. "Interactive Learning in the Classroom: Is Student Response Method Related to Classroom Performance?" *Teaching of Psychology* 38 (3): 147–150. doi:10.1177/0098628311411789.

Elliot, A. C., and W. A. Woodward. 2007. *Statistical Analysis: Quick Reference Guidebook with SPSS Examples*. Thousand Oaks, CA: Sage.

Field, A. 2013. *Discovering Statistics Using IBM SPSS Statistics, 4e*. Los Angeles: Sage.

Fortner-Wood, C., L. Armistead, A. Marchand, and F. B. Morris. 2013. "The Effects of Student Response Systems on Student Learning and Attitudes in Undergraduate Psychology Courses." *Teaching of Psychology* 40 (1): 26–30. doi:10.1177/0098628312465860.

Greenberg, K. P. 2012. "A Reliable and Valid Weighted Scoring Instrument for Use in Grading APA-Style Empirical Research Report." *Teaching of Psychology* 39 (1): 17–23. doi:10.1177/0098628311430643.

Gurung, R. A. R. 2013. "Getting Foxy: Invoking Different Magesteria in the Scholarship of Teaching and Learning." *Teaching and Learning Inquiry*. Manuscript under review.

Gurung, R. A. R., and B. M. Schwartz. 2009. *Optimizing Teaching and Learning: Pedagogical Research in Practice*. Malden, MA: Blackwell.

Keeley, J., D. Smith, and W. Buskist. 2006. "The Teacher Behaviors Checklist: Factor Analysis of Its Utility for Evaluating Teaching." *Teaching of Psychology* 33: 84–91. doi:10.1207/s15328023top3302_1.

Komarraju, M. 2006. "A Social-Cognitive Approach to Training Teaching Assistants." *Teaching of Psychology* 35: 327–334. doi:10.1080/00986280802374344.

Komarraju, M. 2013. "Ideal Teacher Behaviors: Student Motivation and Self-Efficacy Predict Preferences." *Teaching of Psychology* 40 (2): 104–110. doi:10.1177/0098628312475029.

McCann, L. I., K. R. Immel, T. L. Kadah-Ammeter, and S. J. Priniski. 2013. "Student Grade Expectations at Technical College, 2-, and 4-Year Institutions." *Teaching of Psychology* 40 (3): 228–232. doi:10.1177/0098628313487423.

Neimeyer, G. J., G. A. Lee., J. Saferstein, and Y. Pickett. 2004. "Effects of a Graduate Preparation Program on Undergraduate Psychology Majors." *Teaching of Psychology* 31: 247–25. doi:10.1207/s15328023top3104_42.

Tabachnick, B. G., and L. S. Fidell. 2012. *Using Multivariate Statistics, 6e*. Boston: Pearson.

Wilson-Doenges, G., and R. A. R. Gurung. 2013. "Benchmarks for Scholarly Investigations of Teaching and Learning." *Australian Journal of Psychology* 65: 63–70. doi:10.1111/ajpy.12011.

GEORJEANNA WILSON-DOENGES *is an associate professor of psychology and human development at the University of Wisconsin–Green Bay.*

This chapter discusses Institutional Review Boards (IRBs) as they apply to the SoTL. Specifically, it describes when SoTL projects must receive IRB approval, why they must get IRB approval, the review process, and some special issues of concern with regard to SoTL.

6

Navigating the IRB: The Ethics of SoTL

Ryan C. Martin

Institutional Review Boards (IRBs) review proposed research across a wide variety of research settings. They exist in colleges and universities, hospitals, mental health centers, and a host of other institutions where research is regularly conducted. Their purpose is to ensure that the rights and welfare of human subjects in research are being protected. In this chapter, I will discuss IRBs as they apply to the Scholarship of Teaching and Learning (SoTL). Specifically, I will describe when SoTL projects must receive IRB approval, why it is important to get IRB approval, and the review process itself. Likewise, I will discuss special issues of concern with regard to SoTL.

The first thing people need to recognize about IRBs with regard to the Scholarship of Teaching and Learning (SoTL) is that IRBs were not designed with SoTL in mind. Consequently, most IRB resources focus on biomedical or social-scientific research and ignore the types of research we discuss in this volume. Lack of traditional focus on teaching and learning is often frustrating to researchers who want to investigate teaching techniques or assessment strategies; SoTL researchers may find themselves wading through a series of irrelevant questions (e.g., collection of blood samples and asking personal information about illegal behaviors). The process may feel unreasonably time consuming or even unnecessary to pedagogical researchers.

I should note that IRBs are at a loss as well, given their lack of exposure to SoTL. One colleague's IRB dismissed her saying research in her classroom was academic freedom; not to be reviewed by the IRB. She had to push to get a review, and is glad she did. Because so little has been written on IRBs with regard to SoTL, chairpersons have to interpret and apply federal regulations that were not written with SoTL in mind. Further, cautious chairpersons may become overzealous in applying such regulations given lack of comfort with a less well-known area of research. Of course SoTL research should be reviewed by IRBs and may pose many risks to participants. But IRBs need to be educated on potential risks present in SoTL research and take steps to protect participants, the students in our classes. Sometimes urging the IRB to accept a SoTL proposal for review can help educate the IRB and your institution that SoTL research is "real" research.

Must I Do This?

First, it is important to answer the question most SoTL researchers have when they start a project: Does this project require IRB approval? The answer to this question is both simple and complicated. The simple part is that if you are doing "research" with "human subjects," then yes, you must get IRB approval. However, deciding whether or not your project is "research" and whether or not you are using "human subjects" can be tricky.

Before I go any further, I want to note that different disciplines have different terminology for those who participate in research. In psychology, for instance, we refer to them as "participants." In biomedical research, however, it is more common to refer to people as "subjects." Because the Federal Regulations for the Protection of Human Subjects uses the term "subjects," I will use that term throughout the chapter.

Starting with the human-subjects part of this question, according to federal regulations, a human subject is "a living individual about whom an investigator (whether professional or student) conducting research obtains (1) data through intervention or interaction with the individual, or (2) identifiable private information" (Protection of Human Subjects 2009, 46.102.f). Obviously, students in our classes are living individuals, and we are collecting identifiable private information (or at least data gained from interacting with students). Therefore, students are our human subjects. But what if we are looking at old exams (no contact with people) and have had someone remove names and other identifiers? Can essays or old exams truly have all identifiers removed, or might there be some identifying piece of information in the text? As another example, what if you have collected essays from a variety of other classes in your department and have no access to any names or identifiers? Does this procedure constitute an "intervention or interaction" with the participant?

We see similar complications when trying to define SoTL "research." Federal guidelines define research as "a systematic investigation, including research development, testing and evaluation, designed to develop or contribute to generalizable knowledge" (Protection of Human Subjects 2009, 46.102.d). In other words, if the intention is to publish or present the findings, the project is contributing to generalizable knowledge and would require IRB approval. Just as with human subjects, there is substantial gray area here. How systematic must the investigation be in order to meet the federal definition of research? What constitutes generalizable knowledge? Does, for example, institutional assessment require IRB approval? What if the results from such assessment are included in a university brochure or on the website? Should this be considered research, and should it receive IRB approval?

To complicate matters, different IRBs will often answer these questions differently, leading to frustration from researchers about whether or not a project needs approval. To address this ambiguity, two useful rules will help you make such a determination about your own project. First, if you are collecting data from students with the intention of publishing or presenting the findings, it is likely considered research with human subjects, and you should obtain IRB approval before starting the data collection. Second, if you are unsure whether your project is considered research with human subjects, ask your IRB chairperson for his or her guidance. Collecting data on a research project without obtaining IRB approval can have serious negative consequences to the institution, the researcher, and the participants, and such activity should be avoided at all costs. Soliciting guidance when you are uncertain is the safest course of action.

Why Must I Do This?

A second question that often comes up for researchers is: Why must I do this? The sense from many SoTL scholars is that the research is relatively low risk. Researchers are not taking blood samples, deceiving their participants, or administering electric shocks, for examples. In many or even most cases, SoTL researchers are probably right to define their research as low risk, especially compared to other projects being conducted across campus. However, potential risks in SoTL need to be addressed, and the IRB is charged with protecting participants in all studies. In fact, SoTL research may compromise certain aspects of the student-instructor relationship, making participants in SoTL studies a particularly vulnerable group.

The importance of IRBs is rooted in *The Belmont Report* (National Commission for the Protection of Human Subjects of Biomedical and Behavioral Research 1979), a 1979 report outlining three guiding principles in conducting ethical research with human subjects: respect for persons (treat individuals as autonomous and protect those with diminished autonomy), beneficence (avoid harm and increase possible benefits), and justice (distribute the benefits and burdens of research equally).

The Belmont Report was written in response to a series of horrific research projects where human subjects had been irreparably damaged or harmed as a result of their participation in the study (Jonsen 2005). The most notable of these was the Tuskegee Syphilis Study, a forty-year research project conducted by the United States Public Health Service where hundreds of African American men with syphilis were studied to explore the effects of the disease. They were never told they had syphilis and were never provided treatment. When the existence of the study was brought to national attention in 1972, Congress passed the National Research Act which paved the way for the writing of *The Belmont Report*.

In response to this report, research institutions needed a mechanism by which they could monitor the research being conducted to make sure it lived up to these guiding principles. IRBs became that mechanism. In the end, the reason why SoTL scholars need to go through the IRB is because we recognize that even though the project may be low risk in comparison to other sorts of projects, there are still some particular areas where participants may have diminished autonomy, may be harmed through their participation, or even be overly burdened by their participation. In fact, SoTL scholars have gone so far as to outline an international statement of ethics for pedagogical research reproduced in Table 6.1 (Gurung et al. 2007). As dedicated and ethical SoTL researchers, we should embrace the IRB process as a way to value and protect our participants.

Table 6.1. An International Code of Ethics for SoTL

Preamble

We the members of the International Society for the Scholarship of Teaching and Learning (ISSOTL) subscribe to the principles expressed in the following code. We acknowledge that the guidelines for conducting ethical investigations into teaching and learning demonstrate great variation at the local, national, and international levels and, that our members will also abide by any additional local ordinances and requirements. In particular, each member is also bound to abide by the requirements of his or her institution's own Institutional Review Board (IRB) or equivalent body.

We propose that all disciplines need to acknowledge the need for basic national and international ethical standards in the scholarship of teaching and learning. We believe three major principles of the Belmont Report can be applied to the scholarship of teaching and learning.

Respect for Persons: Students (the research participants) should be treated with autonomy and must be free to decide whether or not to participate in a research study unless archival data are being used or if results are not to be presented publically.

This becomes specifically relevant to the scholarship of teaching and learning because there is great potential for coercion in such research. There are two ways in which coercion can occur within the context of teaching and learning research. First, a potential participant may feel coerced to participate because of the difference in power between the instructor (i.e., researcher) and student (i.e., participant). Here, a student may participate in a research project because he or she fears a negative evaluation as a result of not participating. Second, a potential participant may feel coerced to participate because he or she appreciates or likes the professor. In this case, a student may feel uncomfortable with a particular study but decides to participate because he or she wants to do the researcher a favor. While this second type of coercion may appear on the surface to be less negative than the first type, it still infringes on the participant's right to make an autonomous decision about whether or not to participate and is, therefore, potentially unethical. To address these concerns, it is imperative that researchers take steps to minimize the degree to which potential participants feel coerced into participation. For example, strategies to decrease perceptions of coercion, such as utilizing another instructor's class, having the person responsible for data collection be unknown to the students, and ensuring anonymity can all be used to decrease the potential for coercion. The use of archival information (e.g., student performance from previous years), and research conducted in established or commonly

(Continued)

New Directions for Teaching and Learning • DOI: 10.1002/tl

Preamble (cont.)

accepted educational settings, involving normal educational practices (such as research on regular education strategies), or on the effectiveness of or the comparison among instructional techniques, curricula, or classroom management methods, may be conducted without student consent if results are not to be presented in some sort of public venue (e.g., conference presentations and publication).

Beneficence: Instructors (researchers) must recognize the need to "maximize possible benefits and minimize possible harm" (5).

The need to minimize possible harm is obvious within the context of the scholarship of teaching and learning. However, teaching and learning scholars have a great opportunity to maximize possible benefits as they conduct their research. This is because they can, when appropriate, use their in-class research as a means of educating students about research ethics, methods, and/or even the results of the study. In other words, an instructor could use the process of collecting data as a teaching moment to inform students about the ethics involved in data collection, the process of collecting data, and how the data will be used, and, when possible, can even share with them the results of the study they participated in. Such an approach goes above the call of duty and truly maximizes the benefits to participants.

Justice: Students (research participants) should be the people who most benefit from the research. It would be unethical to research a particular group in excess if that group is not the group that will benefit from the knowledge generated through the research.

This is an area of research ethics that the scholarship of teaching and learning seems to truly shine. Those students who participate in such research are not only likely to benefit from the knowledge gained through the study they are participating in, but are also clearly the beneficiaries of past research on teaching and learning. Given that SoTL presents some challenges more traditional research does not (e.g., course instructors doing the research themselves on students whose grades depend on the instructor), it is critical to elucidate additional protections for students. For example, pedagogical research conducted on ones' own students are best administered by independent sources and the information provided to the instructor after grades are handed in. Assessments used for formative purposes (results being used to change future pedagogy within the same semester/quarter) would best be conducted anonymously.

Source: Gurung et al. (2007).

The IRB Process

The process of submitting research proposals to the IRB differs somewhat from institution to institution. Thus, it is in your best interest to consult with your IRB's website and other resource materials early in the research planning to determine what will be expected of you. A couple of common elements will likely be required: ethics training, submission of your documentation (e.g., ethics training certificate), review and approval from the IRB (required before data collection begins), and follow-up reviews (annual reviews and addendums).

Levels of Review

One of the most difficult parts of the IRB process is determining what level of review your project will require: exempt, expedited, or full-board review.

Ultimately, it will be the IRB's judgment that matters (i.e., the IRB will determine if your project is exempt, expedited, or requires full-board review). However, the IRB chairperson or compliance officer will likely want you to make an initial determination about the status of your proposal upon submission. Again, if you are unsure of the correct category, ask for advice from the IRB chairperson before submitting.

Exempt. Regarding exempt research, federal regulations identify six categories (Protection of Human Subjects 2009, 46.101) of research that are "exempt" from IRB review, several of which (numbers 1, 2, and 4) are relevant to many SoTL projects. The other three exemptions are unlikely to be relevant to SoTL work and include (3) surveys of public officials or candidates for public office, (5) research conducted by agency heads that are designed to evaluate the public benefit of service programs, and (6) food quality evaluations.

The first category, in particular, covers a substantial range of classroom research:

> (1) Research conducted in established or commonly accepted educational settings, involving normal educational practices, such as (i) research on regular and special education instructional strategies, or (ii) research on the effectiveness of or the comparison among instructional techniques, curricula, or classroom management methods. (Protection of Human Subjects 2009, 46.101.b.1)

Most SoTL scholars probably would argue that category 1 reflects exactly the type of research they are doing, thus their research should be considered exempt. The problem is that "normal educational practices" can entail very different levels of risk depending on the nature of the study. In fact, "normal" is always open to interpretation. What we often see in SoTL work is the use of more sensitive information (e.g., information from reflection essays and personal comments on discussion forums). The personal nature of this information makes it of higher risk than if data included multiple-choice grades or even final course grades. In other words, the IRB will likely look at a project and make determinations about whether it involves "normal educational practices," how sensitive the data are, and other factors like deception and withholding information from participants (Prentice and Oki 2006).

The second exempt category involves "research involving the use of educational tests..., survey procedures, interview procedures or observations of public behavior" (Protection of Human Subjects 2009, 46.101.b.2) when the data being collected do not contain identifiers. Again, much SoTL work would likely fit into this category but just as with category 1 we have to acknowledge the level of risk associated with the "survey procedures, interview procedures," and so on. Some data or data-collection strategies may be more sensitive than others, and consequently, IRB officials may not consider your project to be exempt (Prentice and Oki 2006).

The final exemption category to be addressed here is exemption number four:

> (4) Research involving the collection or study of existing data, documents, records, pathological specimens, or diagnostic specimens, if these sources are publicly available or if the information is recorded by the investigator in such a manner that subjects cannot be identified, directly or through identifiers linked to the subjects. (Protection of Human Subjects 2009, 46.101.b.4)

This exemption is considered the most problematic of the six (Prentice and Oki 2006). Most often, this exemption is used for research in medical settings where the intention is to explore data that were collected for normal medical practice. For instance, if a researcher wanted to go back and look at every case of a particular illness that had been treated in the last three years to explore the success rate of certain treatment approaches, the research would be considered exempt. Many SoTL scholars argue that educational data should be treated the same way and that reviewing existing data from past classes (e.g., responses to exam questions, content of papers, and so on) should be considered exempt.

For this to be true, two things need to be in place. First, all identifiers need to be removed from the data. The researcher needs to remove names, ID numbers, and so on, from all the data being used in the study before any analyses can begin. Second, the data must have been collected during standard teaching practices (e.g., attendance data, exams grades, and discussion points), with no additional data that were collected purely for research purposes. In other words, it is irresponsible to decide to do a study, collect data, and then go back and say this study meets exemption number four because it uses existing data!

Please note that although a project might be exempt from extensive IRB review, most institutions do not allow the researcher to make that decision on his or her own. The research needs to be reviewed by the IRB initially so it can be determined to be exempt and be certified as such. As with any research project, outside review is crucial. However, once it is determined that the research is exempt, it needs no further review from the IRB. The IRB provides documentation to the researcher that the proposal was reviewed and considered exempt and should be kept on file by the IRB and the researcher.

Expedited.   The next level of review is expedited and is reserved for those studies with no more than minimal risk. Minimal risk is defined by federal regulations as more risk than "the probability and magnitude of physical or psychological harm that is normally encountered in the daily lives, or in the routine medical, dental, or psychological examination of healthy persons" (Protection of Human Subjects 2009, 46.303.d).

NEW DIRECTIONS FOR TEACHING AND LEARNING • DOI: 10.1002/tl

In this instance, "the review may be carried out by the IRB chairperson or by one or more experienced reviewers designated by the chairperson from among members of the IRB" (Protection of Human Subjects 2009, 46.110). In other words, the research protocol does not need to be reviewed by the entire IRB committee. Given the definition of minimal risk, most SoTL research (that is not considered exempt) will fall into this category.

Full-Board Review. As the name implies, full-board review is for research that will need to be reviewed by the IRB committee and not just the chairperson or a designee of the chairperson. Full-board review is reserved for those studies that entail more than minimal risk. It would be somewhat unusual for a study on teaching and learning to hold more than minimal risk. However, there are a handful of procedures used commonly in SoTL projects that may serve to increase the risk above this threshold. For instance, some IRBs consider the following to increase risk above minimal: inclusion of participants who are minors (i.e., under eighteen years old), video-taping or audio-taping participants, asking embarrassing or compromising questions (e.g., time spent studying and incidence of cheating), and providing some participants with benefits not available to others (e.g., course credit). These procedures may be used in SoTL projects, and some IRBs consider them risky enough for full review.

Researcher's Rights

Regardless of whether your research proposal is being reviewed by the full IRB or just the chairperson, you as a researcher have rights. For the most part, the IRB is only to review the risks posed by your study to the participants involved. In that sense, the IRB should avoid criticizing your writing, your methodology, or the value of your research. That said, for some higher risk studies, the IRB needs to weigh the potential benefit of the research versus the potential risks. For instance, if the study is high risk and has obvious methodological flaws that diminish the potential benefit of the research, the IRB should take flaws into consideration. Likewise, if the study is high risk, and the researcher does not adequately demonstrate the value of the project in the proposal, the IRB can ask the researcher to offer stronger evidence of the study's value. The IRB does not have license to dismiss research simply because committee members or the chairperson do not value the topic area (i.e., they cannot reject research because they do not value SoTL work). If you feel that your proposal was rejected unfairly, contact the chairperson or request to attend the next IRB meeting.

Researchers also should know that although the IRB chairperson can approve a study on his or her own (if exempt or expedited), he or she cannot reject a study without board review. In other words, if a chairperson does not believe a research projects meets the federal regulations, he or she can move it to the full board to be reviewed. In fact, in full-board reviews, the chairperson has only one vote. This fact helps protect a researcher who may be at odds with an IRB chairperson.

Special Issues of Concern with the Scholarship of Teaching and Learning

In addition to the complications in determining what level of review a particular study requires, other potential IRB issues are particular to SoTL. In this section, I discuss three prevalent issues: timing of research, coercion, and obtaining informed consent.

Timing of Research.   One problem that plagues the scholarship of teaching and learning is the fact that many IRBs, particularly those at smaller academic institutions, do not meet in the summer when the members are not under contract with the institution. At some schools, the chairperson may review exempt or expedited proposals during the summer, but the full board may not meet. This limitation is an obvious problem for all research, but it is particularly complicating for the scholarship of teaching and learning, because SoTL research often needs to begin on the first day of classes.

For example, perhaps the purpose of a study is to track attitude changes over the semester, and the researcher wants to collect data on the first day of class and compare it to the last day of class. Or perhaps a researcher wants to compare responses to a question from the first day of class to that same question on the last day of class. In both of these cases, the researcher would need to have IRB approval before the study could begin. If the study was planned for the fall semester, and the IRB had not met over the summer, it is likely that the proposal could not be reviewed.

Of course, this is not a problem if the researcher knows well in advance that he or she intends to run a project and plans ahead. For many, though, that is not the case. Often, researchers use their summers to make research plans and want to launch studies right away when classes resume in the fall. There are a few ways this problem can be addressed. First, be aware of when your IRB meets and try to plan ahead. Second, consult with your IRB chairperson. Find out if he or she reviews research in the summer, if the full board meets in the summer, and whether a particular project would require full-board review or not. Further, if summer review is not an option, find out whether or not the chairperson would be able to review the project right away when the fall semester starts to avoid a delay in the research. Third, make adjustments to your research if need be. If summer review is simply not a possibility, look at your research protocol to see if it is possible to delay the initial data collection without negatively influencing the study. In some cases, minor adjustments will address the problem. Finally, do not collect data without IRB approval. Doing so is a violation of federal policy and likely violates your institution's policies as well.

Coercion. One issue that is particularly salient with the Scholarship of Teaching and Learning is whether or not participants feel free to withdraw from a study or to not even participate in the first place (Swenson and McCarthy 2012). There are two ways that this sort of coercion can happen in SoTL work. First, coercion may occur through a direct benefit to participating such as course credit. Students need course credit, so they will feel pressured to do the study. Second, because SoTL researchers often have an instructor-student relationship with their potential participants, students may feel undue pressure to participate in the study to gain their instructor's approval. In fact, perhaps a student feels that he or she should participate because refusing to participate might negatively affect a grade. As an alternative, perhaps a student might feel pressure to participate because he or she is interested in being the professor's research assistant and worries the teacher will hold a grudge if participation does not occur. In any of these cases, the participant has been coerced, albeit unintentionally, to participate in the study.

You can address these potential issues in several ways. First, when you offer course credit (including extra credit) for participation, be sure to offer an equivalent alternative to participation. To be equivalent, the option should take approximately the same amount of time and offer the same potential learning value to the student. For instance, if you have students complete a survey on their attitudes toward the course as part of a research project, perhaps an alternative is a short essay that will not be used in the study. In the essay, students can reflect on their experience with the course. A second way to minimize the possibility of students feeling coerced into participation is to develop a system by which you do not know who chose to participate and who did not. For example, in some projects it might be possible for a colleague who is unaffiliated with the research project to attend class for data collection and keep the data and consent forms until after grades have been submitted. Likewise, it might be possible to utilize online data-collection software that will make it impossible for you to know who did and did not choose to participate. Regardless of how you assure anonymity, you need to let students know your plan; otherwise they may have no idea that data (and participation) will be anonymous. Taking steps to minimize potential pressure to participate could go a long way toward reducing the risk of coercion.

Obtaining Informed Consent. Obtaining informed consent is one of the most important aspects of research with human subjects. The need to do so is rooted in one of the basic principles of *The Belmont Report*, "respect for persons." It is also the element of IRB review process where the IRB is mostly likely to have questions or to ask for clarification (Gillespie 1999).

With exception to some very rare circumstances outlined in the federal regulations (Protection of Human Subjects 2009, 46.116), participants must always give consent to participate in the study. Typically, informed consent requires that participants be told the purpose of the study, potential risks associated with the study, the benefits to participating in the study, a disclosure of alternative options to participating in the study, and other pertinent information (e.g., how data will be used, confidentiality, and reminder that the study is voluntary).

Under certain circumstances, however, documentation of informed consent is not needed. Specifically, researchers do not need to obtain a signed consent form if the research "presents no more than minimal risk of harm to subjects" (Protection of Human Subjects 2009, 46.117.c2) or when "the only record linking the subject and the research would be the consent document and the principle risk would be potential harm resulting from a breach of confidentiality" (Protection of Human Subjects 2009, 46.117.c1). In this second instance, participants should be asked if they want to sign a consent form or not. Keep in mind, though, that in both of these circumstances, subjects must be informed of the nature of the study and consent must still be obtained. The researcher would still provide the information to participants (verbally, in writing, or both). The subject "consents" by the act of completing the survey or participating in the study (without necessarily signing a form). In other words, the IRB is not waiving the informed-consent requirement. Instead, the IRB is waiving the requirement of documentation by not requiring the participant to sign a consent form.

As mentioned to above, there are circumstances when a researcher does not need to obtain informed consent. These circumstances are outlined in the federal regulations (Protection of Human Subjects 2009, 46.116.d):

An IRB may approve a consent procedure which does not include, or which alters, some or all of the elements of informed consent set forth in this section, or waive the requirements to obtain informed consent provided the IRB finds and documents that:

1. The research involves no more than minimal risk to the subjects;
2. The waiver or alteration will not adversely affect the rights and welfare of the subjects;
3. The research could not practicably be carried out without the waiver or alteration; and
4. Whenever appropriate, the subjects will be provided with additional pertinent information after participation.

As all four of these requirements must be met, there may not be many SoTL projects that would meet this requirement. However, an applicable study might include naturalistic observation of how students participate in class. Or a study might compare performance of students who sit in the front of the room to those who sit in the back of the room. In both of these cases, obtaining consent would alter the results, as students would perform differently if they knew the study was being conducted. Thus, "the research could not practically be carried out without the waiver" of consent. Research meeting these four circumstances likely is rare in SoTL and, as a general rule, it is better to obtain consent. Furthermore, the IRB is the body that decides if the circumstances are met.

In Conclusion: Some Final Tips

1. Read *The Belmont Report*: Ultimately, *The Belmont Report* is the seminal work on research ethics in the United States, and those who plan research using human subjects should read it before starting their work. In fact, some IRBs will actually require researchers to read the report prior to proposal submission.

2. Consult with your IRB website: Different IRBs operate differently when it comes to procedures for review, frequency of meetings, and so on. As you start to plan your research, take a look at the IRB website to get a feel for how the IRB operates. Find out how often the full board meets, when those meetings occur, how long the chairperson may need to review your research, what paperwork must be filed, and other relevant information. Planning ahead of time may save you some frustration later.

3. When unsure of something, consult with the chairperson of the IRB: The IRB chairperson is not simply in office to review and approve research protocols. He or she should also serve as a consultant for researchers who have questions about the ethics of their research and how to address certain ethical concerns that may arise. If you have questions about your research (e.g., the level of review required, whether or not certain procedures are acceptable), an easy solution is to ask the IRB chairperson for his or her opinion.

4. Think about the process from the IRB chairperson's perspective: Researchers sometimes complain that the IRB process is unnecessarily bureaucratic and time consuming. There may be times when both accusations are true, but I would urge you to remember one thing as you go through the process: The IRB chairperson's job is to ensure that the research being conducted at the institution is done in a way that protects the rights of and minimizes potential harm to research participants. If someone is harmed though participation in an IRB-approved research project, the chairperson of the IRB may be fully or partially culpable. In this sense, IRB chairpersons are tasked with an exceedingly important set of responsibilities, and it is in everyone's best interest if they are diligent and thoughtful in their work.

5. Know your rights as a researcher: Despite the enormous responsibility of the IRB chairperson, it is possible that he or she, or even a full board, can be overzealous. Remember, as described earlier, researchers have rights too. It is important for researchers to be aware of those rights in order to avoid delays due to an overzealous IRB.

In summary, despite the obvious importance of the Scholarship of Teaching and Learning, such research is not benign from an ethical-risk perspective, and care should be taken as SoTL research is conducted. This chapter highlights the relevant federal regulations and important aspects of the IRB process as well as provides strategies for conducting research in an ethical manner.

References

Gillespie, J. F. 1999. "The Why, What, How, and When of Effective Faculty Use of Institutional Review Boards." In *Protecting Human Participants: Departmental Subject Pools and Institutional Review Boards*, edited by G. Chastain and R. E. Landrum, 157–177. Washington, DC: American Psychological Association.

Gurung, R. A. R., R. C. Martin, P. Jarvis, and G. Creasey. 2007, July. "Code of Conduct: Internationalizing the Ethics of SoTL." Poster presentation at the Fourth Annual Convention of the International Society for the Scholarship of Teaching and Learning, Sydney, Australia.

Jonsen, A. R. 2005. "On the Origins and Future of the Belmont Report." In *Belmont Revisited: Ethical Principles for Research with Human Subjects*, edited by J. F. Childress, E. M. Meslin, and H. T. Shapiro, 3–11. Washington, DC: Georgetown University Press.

National Commission for the Protection of Human Subjects of Biomedical and Behavioral Research. 1979. *The Belmont Report: Ethical Principles and Guidelines for the Protection of Human Subjects of Research*. Washington, DC: U.S. Government Printing Office.

Prentice, E. D., and G. S. F. Oki. 2006. "Exempt from Institutional Review Board Review." In *Institutional Review Board: Management and Function*, edited by E. A. Bankert and R. J. Amdur, 93–96. Sudbury, MA: Jones and Bartlett Publishers.

Protection of Human Subjects. 2009. 45 C.F.R. 46.

Swenson, E. V., and M. A. McCarthy. 2012. "Ethically Conducting the Scholarship of Teaching and Learning Research." In *Teaching Ethically: Challenges and Opportunities*, edited by R. E. Landrum and M. A. McCarthy, 21–29. Washington, DC: American Psychological Association.

RYAN C. MARTIN *is an associate professor and the chairperson of the psychology department at the University of Wisconsin–Green Bay.*

7

This chapter gives reasons why writing is important, summarizes general writing guidelines common to many academic disciplines, and provides specific writing guidelines that authors should use to make their manuscripts stronger and more likely to be acceptable to editors.

Tell a Good Story Well: Writing Tips

Randolph A. Smith

I would wager that everyone reading this chapter has received admonition to become a better writer or at least has wished that he or she could become a better writer. However, I would also wager that many people reading this chapter received little, if any, formal instruction in good writing since the time they were enrolled in English composition courses in college. Readers may have had the obligatory term paper assignment in various undergraduate and graduate courses and probably wrote theses and dissertations, but most writing instruction after the early years of college probably took the form of APA or Chicago-style instruction. There seems to be an implicit assumption that graduate training will magically turn people into good writers, somewhat similar to the idea that graduate training will make people good teachers. This latter assumption has been called into question, as more and more graduate programs are providing explicit and in-depth training in teaching for graduate students (Beers, Hill, and Thompson 2012). The time has come for writing to receive the same type of attention.

Does good writing actually exist in academia? If you have spent much time reading journal articles in your discipline, you may have become almost numb to this question. Journal articles (at least some that I have read in psychology) can be so poorly written that they are difficult to slog through. In introducing my research methods students to reading journal articles, I often joke and tell them not to read their articles late at night when they are tired ... or that they *should* read the articles late at night if they are having trouble falling asleep. Roediger (2007) opined that writing journal articles is one of the most critical skills for academic psychologists. However, it is also a difficult skill to master. In this chapter, I will provide some background information about the quality of writing as it currently exists and provide some pointers to assist the reader in improving writing skills.

New Directions for Teaching and Learning, no. 136, Winter 2013 © 2013 Wiley Periodicals, Inc.
Published online in Wiley Online Library (wileyonlinelibrary.com) • DOI: 10.1002/tl.20077

Is good writing actually important? I strongly suspect that most researchers who are working on a journal article would say yes to this question, but they firmly believe that the actual topic and data are far more important than the writing. Northam et al. (2010) designed a survey for editors of nursing journals (sixty-three respondents) to help determine the relative importance of various aspects of submitted manuscripts. The survey allowed the journal editors to list up to three reasons as to why they rejected manuscript submissions. Figure 7.1 summarizes Northam and colleagues' results. "Poorly written" was the most frequently chosen reason for rejection by the editors (35.8 percent overall), as it had the highest percentage of choices as the first, second, and third most popular reason. Close behind poor writing was the problem of "topic not relevant to the journal" (32.8 percent overall), with "methodology problems" (16.4 percent overall) a distant third choice of the editors for rejecting a manuscript. If Northam et al.'s (2010) findings are generalizable beyond nursing journals, then, yes, good writing is not only important, it is critical for authors who are seeking to publish their articles in journals.

In psychology, faculty may fail to address writing even when training students in the discipline. Psychology departments pay considerably more attention to research and statistics than to writing. For example, Perlman and McCann (1999) studied psychology curricula in 400 college catalogs and compiled a list of the thirty most frequent courses in undergraduate programs; they also included comparative data from similar studies published between 1961 and 1975. Although statistics and research/experimental courses appeared high on the list (numbers ten and thirteen, respectively), there were no courses specifically addressing writing on the list at any of the survey periods. Using slightly different methodology, Stoloff et al. (2010) examined curricula of 374 undergraduate programs and found that 100 percent offered courses in the research methods/statistics area. However,

Figure 7.1. Top Reasons Given by Nursing Journal Editors for Rejecting Manuscripts

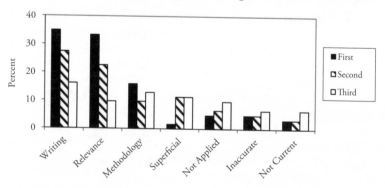

writing again did not appear in the top thirty listed course areas. In fact, the word "writing" did not even appear in Stoloff and colleagues' article. Results similar to both sets of findings also appeared in a Department of Education report (Adelman 2004). Although a 2013 Google search did turn up "writing in psychology" courses at a few institutions (e.g., University of Florida, University of Illinois at Chicago, Penn State), such courses are rarities. It is quite likely that the contrast between research and writing instruction is even more pronounced at the graduate level in psychology. Thus, most authors probably do not pay as much attention to their writing as they do to the other aspects of compiling the research paper. This situation should seem ironic, given that the purpose of the research report is to clearly communicate about one's research. "Authors of scientific articles contribute most to the literature when they communicate clearly and concisely" (American Psychological Association 2010, 9). Looking further at Adelman's data, it should come as no surprise that English Composition was the most-taken college course by students who graduated from high school in 1972, 1982, and 1992. However, there may be a disconnect between student writing in English Composition and what the courses in their major require. For example, some of the literary devices that are popular in English composition courses are frowned upon in disciplines that require scientific writing.

Sword (2012) published an analysis of academic writing and provided interesting insights into some of the issues involved. She too noted that there is precious little instruction in writing provided for graduate students, saying, "For most academics, formal training on how to write 'like a historian' or 'like a biologist' begins and ends with the PhD, *if it happens at all*" (24, emphasis added). She pointed out that, after graduate school, academics have three possible sources of feedback about their writing: memories of what their dissertation advisors told them, comments from reviewers on manuscripts that they submit for publication, and reading articles published by other researchers. However, Sword wrote that all three of these sources tended to maintain the status quo with regard to writing: "Academics who learn to write by imitation will almost inevitably pick up the same bad habits" (24).

General Writing Guidelines

Sword (2012) was curious as to whether sources about good writing existed that could serve as supplements to the three previously mentioned sources. She examined one hundred writing guides aimed at academic writers (e.g., Strunk and White 2000; Williams 2007). She was particularly curious to determine whether there was potential overlap in advice offered by these guides as well as how they aligned with actual practice in academic writing. Sword found virtually unanimous agreement in the various writing guides about six pieces of writing advice (26–27):

1. Clarity, coherence, concision
2. Short or mixed-length sentences
3. Plain English
4. Precision
5. Active verbs
6. Telling a story

Given that Sword (2012) extracted information from a wide variety of writing guides, one important question is whether these six points are consistent with American Psychological Association (APA) style, as published in the *Publication Manual* (*PM*; APA 2010). Therefore, I searched the *PM* to determine whether it contains the same or similar information. Of course, similar searches could focus on MLA or Chicago styles; because of my background, I focused on APA style. Although I refer to the sixth edition of the APA manual in this chapter, these writing guidelines have been consistent through many editions of the manual. Not surprisingly, the *PM* does contain information that is quite consistent with Sword's findings.

Clarity, Coherence, and Concision.   Given that Chapter 3 of the *PM* is titled "Writing Clearly and Concisely," it is apparent that this point receives considerable attention in APA style. "The prime objective of scientific reporting is clear communication" (APA 2010, 65). Clarity receives particular attention in Section 3.09 (Precision and Clarity), with strong focus placed on word choice, colloquial expressions, jargon, pronouns, comparisons, and attribution. Perhaps the most representative admonition within this section is to "make certain that every word means exactly what you intend it to mean" (APA 2010, 68).

The *PM* emphasizes coherence in Sections 3.05 (Continuity in Presentation of Ideas) and 3.06 (Smoothness of Expression). The *PM* urges continuity "in words, concepts, and thematic development" (APA 2010, 65) from the beginning to the end of a manuscript. Such continuity will result in a much clearer manuscript than one that meanders through the topic, making the reader struggle to find a coherent message. Regarding smoothness of expression, the *PM* suggests that authors eschew literary devices commonly found in creative writing, such as ambiguity, surprise, and sudden shifts. Although such writing may make for pleasurable fiction reading, it is disconcerting within a scientific paper.

Section 3.08 (Economy of Expression) emphasizes concision: "Say only what needs to be said" (APA 2010, 67). Items of focus within this section include wordiness, redundancy, and unit length. There are several good arguments for being concise in scientific writing. For example, journals have limited pages with which to work. Thus, when asking for revisions, editors often request that authors condense their manuscripts. In my 14+ years of journal editing, my phrase to express this problem was "authors write more than they have to say." Concise writing is typically easier for readers to comprehend; a common complaint of undergraduate students attempting to read journal articles is that they get lost in all the details and verbiage, some of which is unnecessary. Although technical terminology is often a requirement for scientific writing, writers should remember that, just as in teaching, it is a simple matter to confuse a reader but it may be difficult to make things clear. According to Einstein, "Most of the fundamental ideas of science are essentially simple, and may, as a rule, be expressed in a language comprehensible to everyone" (Einstein and Infeld 1938, 29).

Short or Mixed-Length Sentences.   The PM also covers length of sentences, as well as words and paragraphs, in Section 3.08 (Economy of Expression): "Short words and short sentences are easier to comprehend than are long ones" (APA 2010, 67). Although the PM does warn against using exclusively short words, sentences, and paragraphs, the admonition against being overly long, detailed, and redundant in scientific writing comes through loud and clear in this section. In this section, the PM provides a guideline that a paragraph is probably too long if it is longer than a single double-spaced page.

Plain English.   Section 3.07 (Tone) of the PM deals with this idea. A technique recommended in this section is to write a manuscript with a specific person in mind, trying to inform that person. For example, writing to a researcher in a related field is suggested. Such a person would be interested in keeping up with the literature but would likely be unfamiliar with the nuanced vocabulary or the various perspectives of this literature. Additionally, Section 3.08 (Economy of Expression) specifically mentions avoiding jargon and overly detailed descriptions as ways of shortening long manuscripts and improving their focus.

Precision.   Section 3.09 (Precision and Clarity) addresses this issue with six specific guidelines: word choice, colloquial expressions, jargon, pronouns, comparisons, and attributions. Earlier, I quoted from the PM regarding word choice. Several of the examples in this section relate to writing in the manner of speaking (e.g., using "feel" rather than "think" or "believe"; APA 2010, 68). It may be a simple matter to notice informal writing that sounds more like speech from other writers than in our own writing, but we should closely examine our writing for this problem. In an attempt to avoid this type of informality, however, some writers lapse into an overreliance on complex terms or jargon.

Although pronouns can be helpful in spoken language or casual writing, using pronouns in precise writing can be problematic because the referent for the pronoun is not clear from the writing. Similarly, written comparisons can be confusing when the comparison is ambiguous or illogical. The PM guideline on attributions notes that attempting to be overly objective can lead to problems with attributions, such as using third person, anthropomorphism, or the editorial "we."

You are probably familiar with the word "smith," as in blacksmith or silversmith. According to dictionary.com, one of the root words for smith means "skilled worker." By attempting to write carefully, thinking about words and meanings as they craft their writing, good writers are known as wordsmiths. If you pay close attention to precision in your writing, you will be working at becoming a wordsmith.

Active Verbs. The PM indicates a preference for active voice rather than passive voice within two sections: Sections 2.04 (Abstract) and 3.18 (Verbs). "Verbs are vigorous, direct communicators" (APA 2010, 77). Writing in the passive voice negates this description of what verbs do (or should do). Writing in passive voice often turns an object in a sentence into a subject: "A memory test was given to the participants." Note that there is no actor in this example—the memory test serves as the subject of the sentence, but it did not *do* anything. The possible actors for this sentence would be an experimenter ("The experimenter administered a memory test to the participants.") or the participants themselves ("The participants completed a memory test."). The latter two sample sentences are more direct and more informative than the passive voice construction.

In addition, Strunk and White (1979) noted that brevity is frequently a byproduct of using active voice. Given that page counts and manuscript length are frequently major emphases for academic writing, brevity is a beneficial consequence of writing well. I will return to the "curse" of passive voice soon.

Telling a Story. Information under the header "Writing Style" (APA 2010, 65) emphasizes the importance of engaging the reader in the manuscript: "Establishing a tone that conveys the essential points of your study in an interesting manner will engage readers and communicate your ideas more effectively" (65). In my experience, writing a literature review or introduction to an empirical study are examples of writing that are sorely in need of this guideline. If you read a survey of literature that is simply a listing of one study after another, you get no sense of where the author is headed or what the main point of the review is. My students especially struggle with this problem in compiling literature reviews—although all their studies are linked because of the shared topic, there is no clear development of a story about that topic.

To tell a story well, it must flow smoothly and continuously; the reader must be able to discern your pattern of thinking about the topic. To help you inform the reader about your train of thought, you should focus closely on your transitions—they are critical to the flow of a manuscript. For a literature review, the link between studies is crucial. As I tell my students, as a writer, you must make it clear how Study A led to Study B; how Study C evolved from Study B. Without such transitions, the reader gets the sense of reading about studies that deal with similar topics, but that are randomly arranged.

Roediger's Writing Tips. Roediger (2007) wrote about important considerations for psychologists in authoring empirical journal articles. Several of his points dovetail well with items already mentioned. For example, Roediger urged authors to "Tell a good story" (39) so that readers will be interested and remember what they have read.

Some of Roediger's (2007) admonitions fit well with the guidelines about clarity, coherence, and concision, as he advised authors "Don't have too many subplots" (39), "Short is better (in general)" (40), and "Beware the curse of knowledge" (41). Roediger suggested dividing a manuscript with several subplots into smaller segments, presumably more than one manuscript. Roediger endorsed having briefer sentences, paragraphs, and entire sections of the paper in order to attract readers. Roediger addressed clarity and coherence in his point about the curse of knowledge. He accurately noted that a manuscript is often much clearer to the author than to the reviewers. As authors, we know and understand our arguments and various points better than anyone else—thus, we see clarity in our writing when others may see only muddiness. One of the best cures for this problem is to have a trusted colleague read your writing before you submit it to a journal. Reviewers are typically not amused by papers that are vague and lack clarity. Polishing a manuscript before you submit it is a valuable use of your time.

Roediger (2007) addressed the guideline of using plain English with his admonition to "Avoid excessive abbreviations and acronyms" (41). He likened the use of abbreviations and acronyms to forcing the reader to learn a code at the beginning of a paper and then to use it throughout the paper. As Roediger pointed out, "your prose is much more easily comprehended when you write in words" (41).

Specific Writing Guidelines

I have taught courses in research methods and experimental psychology for over thirty-five years; I have read many student papers during that time. In addition, I served as editor of *Teaching of Psychology* for twelve years, a time during which I read over 3000 manuscripts written by faculty. I also edited *The Psi Chi Journal of Undergraduate Research* for three years, reading many manuscripts from the best and brightest psychology majors. In all of these roles, I have found myself commenting on writing as much as I have the actual content of the manuscripts. From this experience, I share some pointers that faculty and students can use to improve their writing.

Avoid Writing More Than You Have to Say.   This problem is one that typically afflicts faculty writers more than student writers. Several of the pointers I have previously covered have emphasized the value of brevity in one's writing. This tip is an especially valuable one for writing for publication. When writing a manuscript for a journal submission, authors should realize that journal pages are precious commodities. Not only must editors find good manuscripts to publish, they must also ensure that those manuscripts fit within the page limits of the journal. Journals have contracts with publishers that mandate how many pages they can publish in a year—editors cannot simply decide to publish more pages without (typically) incurring financial repercussions. Thus, an editor's job not only entails making decisions about which manuscripts to publish, but also about how long those manuscripts should be.

I often found that authors wrote longer manuscripts than were necessary. I developed a rule of thumb—most manuscripts could be shortened by 20 percent without sacrificing any of the important points that the author wanted to make. My advice to authors was similar to that of Roediger (2007): concentrate on writing briefer sentences, paragraphs, and sections of your manuscript. For some reason, many authors (students included) believe that writing long, convoluted sentences embodies scientific writing. Nothing could be further from the truth: your goal should be to communicate, not to obfuscate. The PM (APA 2010, 61) specifically states that "discursive writing often obscures an author's main points, and condensing long manuscripts often improves them."

During my career as an academic, I have heard many commencement (and similar) speakers who have voiced some variation on Franklin D. Roosevelt's famous advice to his son about how to give a speech: "Be sincere, be brief, be seated" (Soper 1949, 14). This comment is invariably met with applause and laughter—most likely because of the middle guideline of brevity. I suspect that many readers would likewise applaud if writers would follow the same guideline. As you write, focus on telling your story with a minimum of frills and then stop writing.

Avoid Passivity in Your Writing.   The grammatical problem that I mark on manuscripts with the greatest frequency is what I label PV … passive voice. Passive voice involves the use of "be" verbs as helping verbs, resulting in constructions such as "was given" or "were instructed." In this case, the actor is often removed from the sentence and becomes nonexistent. For example, in a manuscript I might read "Subjects were given a recall test." Clearly the subjects did not administer a recall test to themselves—presumably there was an experimenter involved. Using passive voice results in writing that is indirect, more difficult to read and interpret, and often overly wordy.

Just as with wordiness, I believe that the use of passive voice comes from a mistaken impression about scientific writing. Writers seem to be almost paranoid about making direct attributions in their writing and, therefore, strive to avoid doing so. By writing in an indirect manner, authors believe that they are being objective and dispassionate and, thus, scientific in their approach. However, the PM (APA 2010, 69) specifically addresses attribution: "Inappropriately or illogically attributing action in an effort to be objective can be misleading." Using passive voice to avoid attribution is, therefore, a problem.

Fortunately, the solution to avoiding passive voice is relatively simple: use active verbs. This advice was one of Sword's (2012) six major points.

As Strunk and White (1979) noted, active voice is direct and more vigorous than passive voice. This combination will result in prose that is easier and more interesting to read. An added benefit is that writing in active voice also usually results in briefer writing, which is beneficial for publication purposes.

Use the Proper Word(s) in Your Writing.   In APA style specifically, and scientific writing generally, it is vital to write with clarity and precision. One specific manner in which using APA style should ensure clear and precise writing is through the use of words with specific meanings.

Temporal Words.   APA style (APA 2010, 83–84) relegates the words "since" and "while" to temporal (time-related) references. In other words, you should use "since" in your writing only to refer to time after a specific event (e.g., "Since 2010, many researchers have come to the same conclusion,") and "while" to refer to simultaneous occurrences (e.g., "While they were completing the math task, subjects heard white noise played through speakers.").

Many writers use "since" and "while" in the manner in which many people speak; "since" substitutes for "because" and "while" substitutes for "although" or "whereas." According to APA style guidelines, these usages are incorrect. Because APA style places a premium on clarity in writing, you should use "since" and "while" only in the temporal sense of those words.

That/Which.   According to APA style (APA 2010, 83), authors should not use "that" and "which" interchangeably—again, this confusion is a common usage that arises in speech. "That" is appropriate to use for restrictive clauses, which means that the information in the clause is vital to the meaning of the sentence (e.g., "The test that participants completed first was a math achievement test."). In this example, note that removing the restrictive clause ("that participants completed first") renders the sentence meaningless. A restrictive clause restricts the meaning of the sentence in some way.

On the other hand, you should use "which" only for nonrestrictive clauses. The information in nonrestrictive clauses is not vital for understanding a sentence—rather, it is more like an "oh, by the way" comment. The sentence can stand alone and still be meaningful without the inclusion of a nonrestrictive clause (e.g., "The test, which was multiple choice, measured participants' feelings of worth."). In this example, note that removing the nonrestrictive clause retains the important information about the test and retains the key meaning of the sentence—it is critical to know what the test measured rather than the format of the test.

Indefinite Words.   According to the *PM* (APA 2010, 68), "this, that, these, and those" are indefinite words—using them alone could result in a referent that is unclear. Rather than using these words as stand-alone words, they should always precede a noun. Thus, rather than writing about your findings and then using the phrase "These mean that . . . ," you should write

"These results imply that ...." Although you as the writer understand the referent you have in mind, it might be unclear to the reader, which could lead to confusion or misinterpretation. Always using a noun after indefinite words will make your meaning clear to readers.

Revise Well.   Good writers know that they do not do their best writing in their initial drafts. A draft is merely a vehicle for getting your ideas "down on paper" and then giving you something to react to and craft into what you really want to say. People vary in their ability to compose at the keyboard, but editing those first thoughts helps you write a much better paper.

The most common advice I have seen about revising your writing is to put your draft aside for some amount of time—a couple of days to a week is the typical recommendation (Beech 2009; Beins and Beins 2008; Bem 2000; Dunn 2004; Rosnow and Rosnow 2006). The problem with attempting to revise your writing immediately is that you will not have given yourself any time for new ideas to occur and you will likely still be wedded to the words you have written and the wordings you have used. With time comes perspective. As you probably know, critiquing your own work is a difficult task at best—allowing some time away from your article seems to help you become more objective about the task.

An idea that I have used with my students to aid in their editing (echoed by Beins and Beins 2008, 68) is to read your writing aloud. This approach should prevent you from skipping over words or filling in missing information and should help you detect typographical errors, awkward constructions, and grammatical problems.

One key, of course, to revising a paper is to finish a draft well in advance of any deadline that you might be facing. Also, it is important to avoid the risk of feeling a sense of relief in completing a draft and thinking that you have now put another task behind you. Be sure to engage in the revision process; every time that I do, I feel a sense of relief that I had not submitted my first version and been embarrassed by some of the problems I had overlooked.

Conclusion

As everyone reading this chapter knows, the research process is not complete until the researcher shares the results with the scientific community (Smith and Davis 2013). It is incumbent on the researcher to pay careful attention to the writing process: "Authors of scientific articles contribute most to the literature when they communicate clearly and concisely" (APA 2010, 9). If readers have difficulty deciphering an author's writing or draw incorrect conclusions because of poor writing, then an important portion of the research process has gone awry. Be careful as you write—take your time, read your writing carefully, revise, and make certain that your writing says what you intend it to say.

References

Adelman, C. 2004. *The Empirical Curriculum: Changes in Postsecondary Course-Taking, 1972–2000.* Washington, DC: U.S. Department of Education.

American Psychological Association. 2010. *Publication Manual of the American Psychological Association,* 6th ed. Washington, DC: American Psychological Association.

Beech, J. R. 2009. *How to Write in Psychology: A Student Guide.* Malden, MA: Wiley-Blackwell.

Beers, M. J., J. C. Hill, and C. A. Thompson. 2012. *The STP Guide to Graduate Training Programs in the Teaching of Psychology,* 2nd ed. http://teachpsych.org/ebooks/gst2012/index.php.

Beins, B. C., and A. M. Beins 2008. *Effective Writing in Psychology: Papers, Posters, and Presentations.* Malden, MA: Blackwell.

Bem, D. J. 2000. "Writing an Empirical Article." In *Guide to Publishing in Psychology Journals,* edited by R. J. Sternberg, 3–16. Cambridge, UK: Cambridge University Press.

Dunn, D. S. 2004. *A Short Guide to Writing about Psychology.* New York: Pearson Longman.

Einstein, A., and L. Infeld. 1938. *The Evolution of Physics: The Growth of Ideas from Early Concepts to Relativity and Quanta.* New York: Simon and Schuster.

Northam, S., S. Yarbrough, B. Haas, and G. Duke. 2010. "Journal Editor Survey: Information to Help Authors Publish." *Nurse Educator* 35: 29–36.

Perlman, B., and L. I. McCann. 1999. "The Most Frequently Listed Courses in the Undergraduate Curriculum." *Teaching of Psychology* 26: 177–182.

Roediger, H. L., III. 2007, June/July. "Twelve Tips for Authors." *APS Observer* 20 (6): 39–41. http://www.psychologicalscience.org/index.php/publications/observer/2007/june-july-07/twelve-tips-for-authors.html.

Rosnow, R. L., and M. Rosnow. 2006. *Writing Papers in Psychology,* 7th ed. Belmont, CA: Thomson Wadsworth.

Smith, R. A., and S. F. Davis. 2013. *The Psychologist as Detective: An Introduction to Conducting Research in Psychology,* 6th ed. Upper Saddle River, NJ: Pearson.

Soper, P. L. 1949. *Basic Public Speaking.* New York: Oxford University Press.

Stoloff, M., M. McCarthy, L. Keller, V. Varfolomeeva, J. Lynch, K. Makara, S. Simmons, and W. Smiley. 2010. "The Undergraduate Psychology Major: An Examination of Structure and Sequence." *Teaching of Psychology* 37: 4–15.

Strunk, W., Jr., and E. B. White. 1979. *The Elements of Style,* 3rd ed. New York: Macmillan.

Strunk, W., Jr., and E. B. White. 2000. *The Elements of Style,* 4th ed. Needham Heights, MA: Allyn and Bacon.

Sword, H. 2012. *Stylish Academic Writing.* Cambridge, MA: Harvard University Press.

Williams, J. M. 2007. *Style: Lessons in Clarity and Grace,* 9th ed. New York: Pearson Longman.

RANDOLPH A. SMITH *is a professor of psychology at Lamar University.*

8

From the perspective of a journal editor and experienced author, this chapter provides counsel on the "ins" and "outs" of publishing empirical research in peer-reviewed journals.

Navigating the Minefields of Publishing

Andrew N. Christopher

If you are familiar with the TV show *Survivor*, then you are familiar with the trials and tribulations of publishing peer-reviewed work. Although I was never an avid viewer of *Survivor*, it always seemed to me that whatever could go wrong for contestants always did go wrong. Even if you have never submitted a paper for peer review, the fact you are reading this chapter indicates some interest in doing so. Yes, without question, there are horror stories galore about issues authors have had trying to get their work published. However, similar to the likelihood of dying in a plane crash or getting attacked by a killer shark, such publishing horror stories are the exception, not the rule. Don't let the availability heuristic scare you away from trying to publish your work. Getting your work published is rarely easy (and has never been easy in my experiences as an author), but there are some guidelines that I have found, as both an author and an editor, to be extremely helpful in navigating the peer-review process. This chapter will discuss these "rules and regulations" that I find particularly important to follow. Although I am drawing heavily on my experiences as editor of *Teaching of Psychology*, these guidelines should apply to any research that one wants to publish.

There are three sets of guidelines that I provide in this chapter. Each set of guidelines pertains to a distinct stage of manuscript development: (1) before you start writing, (2) as you are writing, and (3) after you have submitted your manuscript.

Before You Start Writing

If you're thinking, "Is there really stuff to do *before* I start writing?" you are not alone in your shock. The most important part of writing is not the writing per se, but rather the preparation and thought that go into preparing to write. That belief is reflected in the fact that of the three major sections of this chapter, preparation is the longest. After you read this section, you

New Directions for Teaching and Learning, no. 136, Winter 2013 © 2013 Wiley Periodicals, Inc.
Published online in Wiley Online Library (wileyonlinelibrary.com) • DOI: 10.1002/tl.20078

will have gained an advantage over many other people in the competition for scarce journal pages.

Before you sit down to write, ask yourself, and more importantly, answer honestly, these questions:

1. What is the purpose of writing this manuscript?
2. Who do you want to read this manuscript?
3. Where, physically, do you prefer to write?
4. When, in terms of time of day and daily schedule, do you prefer to write?
5. What is the length of time you can write in a single sitting?
6. What do you do when you take breaks from writing?

What Is the Purpose of Writing This Manuscript?   There are different purposes in writing a manuscript. Certainly, expanding a knowledge base is something all manuscripts should do. Without question, you must believe in the worth of the manuscript to write it. If you don't believe your idea has intellectual value, just drop it. You're wasting your time trying to write up a manuscript that you don't believe in. I have numerous such papers on my hard drive, the collection of which represents an investment of time and energy better invested almost anywhere else.

At some point, of course, you probably need additional incentive to sustain your writing. For instance, is this paper a potentially integral part of your tenure and promotion package? If so, knowing when those materials are due will help guide you in making a schedule to get the paper from nonexistent to in press (hopefully). Alternatively, perhaps a colleague coauthor more urgently needs a paper to "get out there" for some career milestone. Possibly your manuscript will not help you or a colleague in such a regard, but rather, it is important to your student coauthors in terms of their job prospects or admission to graduate school. Regardless, you need to know what's in it for you, or people whose welfare you care about, to help sustain you through what can be a grinding process. Sometimes getting in the car and driving without a destination can be fun; however, such a mentality is a prelude to failure when starting to write a manuscript.

Who Do You Want to Read This Manuscript?   For less experienced writers, I completely understand and even remember that feeling of "I just want it published, darn it." As an author, I still feel that way about some of my papers. However, it is critical to realize that different journals, even journals whose names might sound similar, serve different purposes. Every journal with which I am familiar contains some sort of "Journal Contents," "Types of Articles," or "Journal Mission" statements. *Please read these statements.* They were crafted for a reason: to attract certain types of articles that the readership of those journals wants to read. For example, *Learning and Individual Differences* (*LID*) and *Teaching of Psychology* (*ToP*) are two outlets that, as you might have guessed from their names, both focus on issues of student learning. Thus, they have more in common with each other than they likely do with many other journals. However, there are some crucial differences between these two excellent journals. For instance, *LID* focuses on individual differences in the educational setting. On the other hand, *ToP* focuses primarily on learning within psychology and has a readership comprising people who teach psychology in some capacity. *LID*'s focus is broader than psychology, with a readership comprising individual-difference and educational researchers in general as opposed to psychology teachers more specifically. Both outlets serve important purposes, but most manuscripts that are appropriate for *ToP* would only be of marginal interest to *LID* readers and vice versa. By knowing at the outset, before you write a single word, the journal or perhaps set of journals that you want your work to appear in, you can focus your writing to appeal to readers of that journal and increase the likelihood it will receive a warm welcome.

Although we will talk about actually writing the manuscript in the next major section, and Smith's chapter in this volume provides more detailed advice on the topic, there is another way to know whether a particular journal may be an appropriate place to submit your work. After you have written your paper, look over your references section. For the articles you cited, are there any journals that tend to pop up in your references a lot? If so, those outlets would be good submission options for you to consider.

Where, Physically, Do You Like to Write?   Let's assume you have a top-notch paper in mind, and you know what and for whom the payoff will be. Therefore, it is worth your time and energy to write your paper. When I get such a realization, my first reaction is to schedule a visit to Panera Bread Company. Yes, seriously. The Panera in Jackson, Michigan, has witnessed many manuscript drafts over the years. For whatever reason, it has emerged as an ideal writing environment for me. Music playing and strangers talking around me is an environment that works well for me when I write. You might think that my school office would be the ideal place to write. Certainly, if I could write while being interrupted seemingly every ten minutes, it would be ideal. I cannot write effectively with what I consider frequent interruptions. In the evenings, however, when there are fewer people around than during the day, my school office becomes a more enticing place to write. Indeed, different places are better for writing at different times of day and on different days of the week. With a little self-observation and reflection, you will find those places and times that are most conducive to productive writing. Sometimes, when preferred writing places are not working for me, I leave as soon as I realize writing won't be happening there. In fact Dana Dunn gave me a particularly excellent piece of advice: If you aren't "into" a task with fifteen minutes of starting it, just move on to something else. Don't stare at it hoping for divine inspiration; that's unlikely to happen. Go find something else to do for a while, and come back to the original task later. You are not giving up and will continue to schedule time for writing.

NEW DIRECTIONS FOR TEACHING AND LEARNING • DOI: 10.1002/tl

When, in Terms of Time of Day and Daily Schedule, Do You Prefer to Write?   Of course, there are only twenty-four hours in the day. Somewhere in there, some writing needs to happen. With an 8 a.m. Introduction to Psychology class this semester, it is unlikely I will do much writing as soon as I wake up. First, for me, 8 a.m. is early. Second, I prefer to get my first class of the day completed before taking on writing tasks. There is something about teaching that helps me engage with the rest of the day (and hence why I agree to do 8 a.m. classes). I could write after class, but I prefer to use the time immediately after class to "clean up" any loose ends from that class meeting and get my materials together for the next class. These are little realizations I have made about myself. It is vital that you make similar self-observations when figuring out when in your daily schedule you can do some writing, Are you a morning person? An evening person? How flexible are you in terms of when you can get mentally challenging work, such as writing, completed? Does teaching energize you to write (as is the case with me) or drain your energy to write (or neither)? Obviously, if you have children or other people to care for, you need to work around their needs as well. Perhaps you even want some time for yourself! That's completely doable too. However, if you are serious about getting writing accomplished, you need to answer these sorts of questions about yourself and lifestyle, then commit to specific times on specific days of the week, and stick with such commitments. Simply saying, "I'll do some writing next week" is a goal unlikely to bear any fruit. Again, waiting for divine inspiration to strike and ignite your writing isn't a good idea. You must be proactive to even have a chance to get your writing done. Even if you take a break after fifteen minutes, doggedly keep that time blocked out for writing and try!

What Is the Length of Time You Can Write in a Single Sitting? This question clearly relates to the previous question. One of my former undergraduates who is now completing his PhD made an interesting observation about one of his writing behaviors. In doing so, he brought attention to one of mine that I had never noticed. He tends to write well from late afternoon into the middle of the evening, normally needing to shut down about 9 p.m. or so. However, on some evenings, he gets rolling, or what we hear athletes call "getting in the zone." When this happens, he simply doesn't stop working; he keeps writing until he cannot write anymore, sometimes pulling an all-nighter. Certainly, if you are a morning person, writing all night may not seem appealing. Again, we all must identify our writing prime time. Even if this time does seem appealing to write, depriving yourself of sleep, especially if you have a class at 8 a.m. the next day, probably does not seem appealing. However, knowing that I tend to be a "binge writer," I am comfortable writing in this same fashion. When I am in the writing zone, I don't want to pull myself out of it.

Relatedly, I find it is often easier to write during the summers than during the school year. Certainly I have heard colleagues at Albion and elsewhere say the same thing. However, to do no writing from late August until early May (the Albion school year) is problematic. When I do my writing during the school year, I tend to do it at night, when daily school-related tasks are less pressing, and I can enter the zone if it strikes me. Every summer, I have at least one manuscript that I intended to complete during the regular school year but only drafted a portion of the paper. Until recently, most of these drafts I mothballed and pulled them out nearly nine months later. Trying to complete these manuscripts was pretty much like writing a manuscript from scratch. It could take a substantial amount of time to revisit and figure out what it is I had done (and why I had done it). To avoid letting such manuscripts fade into the abyss, I knew I had to somehow make time to work on writing during the school year. Although it is easy to say you should block out time each week to devote to writing, putting that intention into practice is far more difficult, especially when there are students who need your attention during that season. However, if you can set and hold yourself to definitive starting and ending times for writing during the school year, it's like saving for retirement; it's amazing how much work can accumulate in relatively small 2–3 hour weekly contributions over an 8–9 month school year! For more ideas about making writing a priority, read Bem's (2004) chapter or Dunn and Zaremba's (1997) article.

What Do You Do When You Take Breaks from Writing?   Although this question will also be considered in the next section of this chapter, consider it before you write too. The prospect of writing can trigger anxiety, knowing that writing will necessarily take time away from of other things that need to get done. The "other things" provide a disincentive to even start writing. To some extent, this fear may be true, but writing does not necessarily mean the rest of your life gets put on hold. I generally write well for about two hours at a stretch, then I start doing too much screen staring. At that point, I need to do something else. For instance, I love coffee. If I am writing at Panera, problem solved. If I am writing at the office at night, there is a departmental Keurig. If I am hiding on campus (locked in my office to work), I can walk over to the campus coffee shop. Taking a break to organize the office or work on materials for a class session are both productive breaks. Likewise, I try to keep my home reasonably clean. If I am writing at home, a quick vacuuming and dusting of the living room is a nice, productive break. Depending on how much writing I've accomplished at the point I need a break, cooking something, even just making something simple such as a Panini sandwich for lunch, is a nice break. Doing other relatively nonmentally draining tasks, such as washing the car, facilitate long-term writing progress, and all of which are productive uses of time.

When it comes to diversions, we all have our weaknesses. Watching an episode of my favorite TV show, *Criminal Minds*, may seem like a good idea for a writing break. However, that hour break is too long for me and makes re-engaging with my writing difficult to do. It is also likely that I will extend that hour break and watch more TV, even if I don't like what's on! Watching perhaps an inning of a Detroit Tigers baseball game may seem like a better idea, but oftentimes, I find myself getting emotionally involved with the team's performance, and again, my mind becomes too far removed from my writing to re-engage effectively with it. I have learned my weaknesses only with experience, and you will need to learn yours. You will need to figure out the best way for you to take breaks from writing. These breaks are an essential part of the process and can help you from feeling like the rest of your life has to shut down to get that writing done. Hopefully this knowledge will stop you from avoiding writing altogether!

You're Almost Ready to Write.   So, now that you've thought through these questions and answered them honestly, here is the most critical activity to the entire writing process, and yes, it happens before you start writing. You must schedule when you will have completed specific parts of the manuscript. This schedule should include the sections of the manuscript and the deadline for each one (at the very least, the introduction, method, results, and discussion sections, but feel free to add in references, tables and figures, and the abstract, and certainly, you can break down these major sections into smaller subsections). To the extent possible, your schedule should include specifically when and where the writing of each section will occur. Certainly, specific times of day for writing may not be possible weeks in advance, but as the time draws near, revise the schedule to include that level of detail. By making your schedule as specific and measurable as possible, you are simply using tried-and-true goal-setting techniques (see Locke and Latham 1990 for a review of goal setting). There will be no gray area as to whether the schedule has been maintained. Consequences for falling behind schedule at certain points (e.g., no chocolate that day), and incentives for keeping up with the schedule at those same points (e.g., an extra piece of chocolate, a manicure, or thirty minutes of a TV show), should be parts of the process.

This schedule should not exist only in your head. It must be put on paper. In fact, put it on multiple pieces of paper, and place those pieces of paper in places you and other people will readily see them. Make use of technology to advertise your schedule; update it on Facebook or use an app such as Wunderlist, a list making tool, to hold yourself accountable to as many people as possible. Tell colleagues, family, and friends alike about your schedule and perhaps give them a copy of it. That way, they can ask you how your manuscript is progressing! I even go so far as to put a copy above my dogs' dinner dishes so they can see it. If I fall behind my schedule, and they are barking at something, it must be they are barking at me for falling behind on that schedule (just kidding, but you get the idea). The power of public commitment is essential for your schedule to help you write. Form or join a writing group with colleagues is another great way to publically commit to your schedule, and doing so can also provide a great deal of interpersonal support in the writing process.

NEW DIRECTIONS FOR TEACHING AND LEARNING • DOI: 10.1002/tl

As You Are Writing

Now for the easy part (yes, really, the easy part). Of the three sections of this chapter, the actual writing is the easiest part! With your preparations completed, your schedule in the hands of trusted people and perhaps paws of trusted pets, you can turn on your computer.

First, the Importance of Humility.   A world of scholars is eagerly awaiting your work, unable to sleep until they devour it. If that's what you're thinking as you start writing, you need to stop it. Yes, there will undoubtedly be people interested in your work. However, don't approach your manuscript as though it will bring about world peace and contain the cures for world hunger and cancer. That's not going to happen. In fact, if the tone of your writing is overly enthusiastic, it will turn off readers no matter what good message you have to convey. Scientific writing is supposed to be objective and unbiased. When a paper reads like an endorsement, it starts to make readers wonder what the writer is trying to hide. Although such zealousness can manifest itself in several ways, I find that drawing conclusions not supported by the data is the most common mistake. Certainly, making causal claims from nonexperimental data is never good. However, when discussing results, making connections to variables that were not measured in the current data happens all too often and detracts from what might otherwise be an important message. Using the word "proves" is problematic, as no one study ever "proves" anything. Rather, a study or set of studies can "suggest" certain conclusions be drawn, with conclusions subject to change in future research. Particularly in applied sorts of research, such as in the scholarship of teaching and learning, when presenting implications, statements such as "A teacher must . . . ," and "It is obvious . . . " are other overly definitive statements that could turn off someone reading your paper with a critical eye. In short, although you can and must feel passionate about the paper you are crafting, such passion should not manifest itself in the paper.

What to Do, What to Do?   Now, with your ego checked at the door, let's start writing. Where to start? Start anywhere, yes, literally anywhere. I always teach my classes the order of the different parts of a manuscript. That does not mean those parts have to be written in that order. Admittedly, making a title page is not difficult to do, and once it's done, I've actually started writing the paper. Something has been accomplished! In terms of substantial writing, I prefer to start with the Method section. This section is the most structured to write; the information it must contain is more proscribed than any other section of the manuscript. So, why not start there? In relatively minimal time, I have a section of the paper drafted.

Now what? I prefer to write as much of the introduction as possible before drafting the Results section. However, my introduction sections tend to be, in early drafts, nothing more than little subsections with no real organization between those subsections. For instance, suppose I am writing a paper about predictors of academic motivation in college students (for examples of such research, see Allen and Robbins 2010; Casillas et al. 2012). I used the Big Five personality factors, Protestant work ethic, and perfectionism as my predictor variables. Certainly, each of these variables needs to be discussed in the introduction. However, do I start the introduction with the academic motivation literature or with the Big Five literature on education-related constructs? I don't know the order of sections when I start writing, so I don't worry about that issue. After I have reviewed and integrated the literature on each of these topics, I can go back and "glue together" my subsections, adding appropriate transitions and segues, of course.

When some researchers conduct a study, they may collect data that fails to yield interesting results. For instance, let's stay with our example of predictors of academic motivation in college students. After thoroughly analyzing your data, you may find that a regression using only the Big Five personality factors tells the most interesting theoretical story and would allow you to most parsimoniously present your data. That being the case, just present results of the regression using the Big Five personality factors as predictors of academic motivation. Don't even mention your Protestant work ethic or perfectionism constructs or the data you collected on them anywhere in your manuscript. They don't exist. It may feel like you are "cheating" readers out of something, but the reality is, presenting data that cloud an otherwise clear picture is only making your picture less attractive. Again, it's not cheating, it's presenting your data in a manner that tells the most interesting and parsimonious story possible (i.e., parsimony is good science).

Also related to presenting results, please be aware that more is not necessarily better in this context. An independent-samples t-test is about the least sexy analysis one can report. Certainly, you could present a regression instead, and doing so could convey the same information. But why not present the results as simply as possible? There are numerous statistical tools that all have important purposes, but fancy statistics don't compensate for a lack of good research ideas or lousy methods to test those ideas. Don't engage in statistical overkill. Doing so may make you feel good about yourself, but it is likely going to confuse readers, and they are the audience of ultimate importance.

Again, this is personal preference, but I cannot draft a discussion section until I have the introduction, method, and results on paper. The discussion is supposed to, by its very name, integrate issues raised in the introduction, addressed with the methods used in the paper, and answered with the results presented. Until those issues are on paper, I find writing discussion sections is not a productive use of my time. However, I do have a most talented colleague who finds writing discussions in tandem with introductions works well for her. More power to her, and to you as well, as each of us must find what works best in terms of when to write each section of our manuscripts.

Some Not-So-Little Things to Keep in Mind.   As you are writing, never forget the journal you are targeting. Keep the mission statement within view as you write. Doing so may help keep you from going off on tangents that the journal readers may not care about. For instance, readers of *LID* would likely want more background information on the Big Five than would readers of *ToP*, who would likely prefer more text about the implications of the results for teaching than the theory driving the research. Never lose sight of the audience you are trying to reach.

In addition to keeping our target audience in mind, we should also expect our writing to adhere to certain standards. Although many of us may lament how poorly our students write, many of us may well be surprised that sometimes authors for journals don't write well either. As both an editor and author, I have reviewed numerous papers that contain multiple sentence fragments, paragraphs that span more than three manuscript pages, and empirical studies described that fail to present any sort of data, to name but three common egregious mistakes. However, even relatively minor mishaps such as missing words in sentences detract from the perceive quality of a manuscript. Adherence to APA format (or whatever style an outlet uses) matters too; even if APA formatting is not perfect, trying to adhere to it demonstrates you are actually serious about publishing in that particular outlet.

We are almost ready to submit a paper for publication! Please do yourself a huge favor, not only now but also at all stages of writing a paper. Save your work often, but more importantly, once you have done what you consider a significant and substantial amount of writing, save your paper under a new file name. Additionally, you could save it using the current date as the file name (e.g., "May 20.2013 MEQ and personality draft 4"). By the time I submit a given manuscript, I usually have 20–25 versions of it as it is being drafted. First, seeing all those files does provide a sense of accomplishment. Second, and more importantly, as that paper gets revised and improved toward its submission, I have copies of previous drafts available to me. When I get feedback from reviewers and the editor, they may well ask me (and oftentimes do) to include text that I may have previously written but deleted from the submitted piece. Or editors may ask for clarification of existing text, and such clarification may exist in a previous draft of the manuscript. We never know when a rough draft may contain a diamond that we just didn't recognize at the time.

Although this might be something you should arrange before you start writing (as part of that publically available schedule you made), have a successfully published colleague read your manuscript and offer commentary—just like the reviewers and editor will do for you. This person might alert you to issues that you could easily miss, particularly with respect to the tone of the manuscript. Some issues this person may raise will be things you can do nothing about. For instance, if you did not collect data on a particular variable, it's too late to do that at this stage of the research.

However, perhaps feedback will help you realize that doing an additional study is a good idea. Why not do it now, and after you get feedback on your current manuscript from the reviewers and the editor, you can integrate new data if needed? Of course, for suggestions that *can* be changed, do so. Keep in mind that if the person reading your paper is unclear about any wording, it is your responsibility as the author of the paper to clarify that text. Don't argue or negotiate such details. If a colleague does not understand something in the paper, the paper is flawed. Period.

After You Have Submitted Your Manuscript

You clicked that "submit" button, and your work is finally finished, right? Wrong! For the time being, yes, there is not a lot you can do on that manuscript, as it is in the hands of the editor and review team. However, for your manuscript to be published eventually, there is more work ahead.

Before we get to what comes next, there is one minor but critical detail you need to attend to. Some journals use a manuscript-processing system, whereas others use email submissions. Regardless, you should receive a confirmation of your submission after submitting it. For some of these manuscript-processing systems, confirmation is an automated response generated when a paper is submitted. For emailed submissions, the editor or editorial assistant should contact you with an acknowledgment. If you do not receive any sort of confirmation within about seventy-two hours, you should email the editor or editorial assistant to make sure all is well with your submission.

How long will it take your paper to be reviewed? The answer to this question is a highly variable one. Journals have an incentive to provide feedback quickly to authors, as journals need papers to publish. That said, yes, here is where many a horror story can be had. Some journals will state in their "contents" sections their approximate review times; others will tell you this information in the acknowledgement when you submit your paper. Others do not provide such estimates. When estimates are provided, editors are sincere. However, please realize that life happens, and review times will vary. The best reviewers are like the best faculty members on your campus; they are asked to do a lot of work! Because they are the best faculty members on their campuses, they are doing a lot in other areas of their professional lives as well. Excellent reviewers are extremely busy people. Editors work 25–30 hours each week simply to obtain feedback from reviewers. All that said, if you've waited more than a month beyond the stated response time, contact the journal. Few if any editors will see you as being a pest for doing so, as long as you are professional in the process.

At some point, hopefully well within the stated response time, you will receive an email with a subject line similar to "decision on your submission." I see such emails and still feel a wave of both excitement and dread. You will find, somewhere in that email, details of whether or not you are invited to revise and resubmit your paper to that journal. Frankly, on your initial submission of a manuscript, you should be happy, if not thrilled, to receive such an invitation. No, an invitation to revise and resubmit is by no means an acceptance of your work, nor does it guarantee you will receive an acceptance of it in the future. However, in my almost five years as editor of *Teaching of Psychology*, the vast majority of published papers were revised. We have accepted a total of four manuscripts for publication on their initial submission. That is less than 0.25 percent of all submissions, and even these four papers required revisions before being issued formal acceptance. In short, on an initial submission, if you receive invitation to revise and resubmit the paper, you have accomplished your goal!

Now, before we talk about how to handle an invitation to revise your paper, let's discuss what to do if you do not receive such an invitation (i.e., if your paper is rejected). First, having a paper rejected does not mean the paper contains no value and will never be published. To take an example from my own experiences, I have published three papers in the *Journal of Social and Clinical Psychology (JSCP)*. All three of these papers had previously been rejected by *Personality and Individual Differences (PAID)*! Both are quality outlets, but apparently some of my work was more appropriate for *JSCP* than for *PAID*. Interesting, I have initially submitted two papers to *JSCP*, and neither received that coveted invitation to revise and resubmit. However, I was able to get them published eventually … in none other than *PAID*! Persistence is important if you want your work published. In fact, much like I found finishing my dissertation was more about persistence than intellectual brilliance, so too is the case with navigating the publication challenge.

If your work fails to get an invitation to revise and submit, find that list of possible journals you were considering when you started writing. Decide on an alternative outlet. Use the information in the reviews you received to decide if in fact your manuscript can be improved. If so, and you have the time and energy available, integrate the feedback from reviewers and the editor, and submit your paper to another outlet. Notice I said "integrate the feedback from the reviewers." Even though you are submitting to a new journal, don't kid yourself. It's a small world when it comes to research. The odds of one of the same reviewers commenting on your paper at this new journal are fairly good (well more than 5 percent, I assure you). If you simply take the same paper and submit it elsewhere and this reviewer realizes his or her work was ignored, expect the worst. Integrate as much of the feedback as possible. Making an honest effort to do so will not only improve the quality of the paper (which is obviously the primary concern) but also reward the reviewers for their efforts on the initial submission.

If you are holding that revise and resubmit invitation, let's talk about what to do now. As you prepare to dive into the reviews, realize that reviewers are people, and people are highly variable in many ways. One way such variability manifests itself is in how people approach reviewing tasks.

Some reviewers may write no more than a couple of paragraphs, focusing on a couple of major issues that need to be addressed before he or she is willing to consider the paper further. This may feel insulting, after all, you did all this work, and someone provided perhaps half a page of feedback. Don't take it personally; focus on addressing those concerns (and perhaps be grateful they did not provide five or six pages of comments, which some reviewers will certainly do!). Other reviewers provide section-by-section commentary. Still other reviewers organize their work from most important issues to address to lesser important point to address. Indeed, there is no "typical review" (the longest review I've even seen was slightly more than eleven single-spaced pages). Some reviewers harp on APA style; others love to copyedit submissions. There is no one way people conduct reviews, so please be able and willing to roll with however the reports on your manuscript are presented.

When revising your manuscript, pay attention to the points raised in the reviews. I am not saying agree with all the points raised in the reviews, but you must consider every single one of them. Much like I don't appreciate it when students don't listen in class, reviewers and editors get annoyed when authors ignore their well-intentioned feedback. I am not saying you must implement every change suggested in the reports, but you must consider them and if nothing else, address them in a cover letter.

You should read the reports at least two or three times before starting to revise the paper. Sometimes suggestions will be made explicit, but other times you need to discern what appear to be the most pressing issues to address in revising the paper. I feel that my job as editor is to highlight in a decision letter those points that are particularly critical to address in a revised paper. I find most editors do the same in their letters. However, I do sometimes receive editorial letters that basically say simply "Address the points raised in the reviews" without any guidance as to their relative importance. Thus, in such circumstances, the author needs to make determinations about importance.

Integrate as many of the reviewer and editor suggestions as you can. That is really the most important part of revising your paper. Again, integrate as many of the reviewer and editor suggestions as you can. When you do not make a suggested change, simply explain in the cover letter why you decided against doing so.

Simple enough, but what happens when you disagree with a suggested change (that you've considered carefully, of course) or simply can't make the change? For example, if you did not collect data on a specific variable, you need to make that point. In this specific example, perhaps you could include this suggestion as a future research direction in your paper. When you revise a paper, always include a cover letter, even if not asked to do so, that explains how you changed the manuscript in light of the feedback provided in the reviews and editor's decision letter. That cover letter may well be as critical to the paper's success as the paper itself. Organize the cover letter around the reviewer and editor feedback. For instance, in the cover letter, explain how you addressed each point raised by each reviewer, and then anything additional raised by the editor. You could even take the file that contains the reviews, then insert under each issue raised how you addressed it, and use that as your cover letter! Regardless of the cover letter format, don't worry about its length. Take as much text in the cover letter as you need to explain why you revised the paper as you did. This is especially important when explaining why you decided *against* making a suggested change. When you must provide an explanation for not making a suggested, address it intellectually, not emotionally. Don't say, "that comment is wrong." Rather, explain why making the change would detract from the message and/or quality of the paper. If at all possible and applicable, cite research that substantiates your argument. For instance, if a reviewer suggests a reanalysis of some or all of the data, and you don't feel such analyses are appropriate, explain your rationale, and if possible, cite research that would argue against the suggested reanalysis.

One particular and widespread suggestion that appears often in reviews and should be discussed in more detail here is the dreaded "collect more data" suggestion. As an editor, I am truly ambivalent when reviewers make this suggestion. Certainly, there is always more data to collect and methodological improvements to be made. In some ways, this comment is almost self-evident. However, when such a suggestion would lead to significant improvement in the paper, then it should be considered seriously. How do you know if additional data collection is a make-or-break issue for your paper? This is one suggestion I *always* bring up in a decision letter. Phrases such as "additional data are essential to the revision's success" or "additional data would greatly enhance the value of this contribution" are clues that this suggestion, as onerous as it may be, needs to be implemented. If I don't feel such additional data are not necessary to the paper's success, I will include text such as "Although additional data would enhance the value of this paper, they may not be a make-or-break issue." Such comments don't preclude collecting more data, but assuming other revisions are implemented well (in the opinions of the reviewers and editor), the additional-data issue won't kill the paper's chances at that outlet.

Some editors will provide a deadline for resubmitting your manuscript, but other editors do not. Regardless, one law of the publication game is to revise and resubmit your work not only as thoroughly as possible but as quickly as possible. When invited to revise and resubmit a paper, that paper immediately becomes a top professional priority. Why is it important to revise and resubmit quickly and thoroughly? If too much time passes between receiving the invitation and revising the paper, the reviewers and editors are more likely to read the revised paper more as a new submission than as a revision. A lengthy revision time allows reviewers and editors to forget the paper, so when it comes back in revised form, they could well comment on things they did not comment on the first time! I've even

NEW DIRECTIONS FOR TEACHING AND LEARNING • DOI: 10.1002/tl

received comments from reviewers, when commenting on a revised paper, that they now disagreed with some of their initial suggestions! Such occurrences are not malicious, but they do happen, typically when a great deal of time has passed since reading the initial submission. In addition, a quick revision demonstrates that you consider this paper to be important. Certainly, reviewers and editors want to publish papers that contain important information. If the paper is so important to you, why did it take you so long to revise it? Do what you can to prevent this from happening to your work. Regardless of whether or not the editor sets a deadline for resubmitting, do it now!

After you resubmit your paper, the waiting begins again. Please understand that the coveted invitation to revise and resubmit is not a guarantee your next email from the journal will be an even-more-coveted acceptance letter. The invitation to revise and resubmit was an indication that you might have something valuable for the readership. When you have submitted your revised paper, the editor may ask the reviewers or a subset of the reviewer team to comment on the revised piece. Some editors may ask a new reviewer to read the revised paper. Finally, some editors may read your revision and make a decision on it without further consulting the reviewers. The next email could very well be another invitation to revise and resubmit; this is a good development! Revise the paper again, doing as much as you can of what was suggested. The number of revisions a journal might request varies widely; some editors will allow one revision and that one revision either gets accepted or rejected. Other editors will allow numerous revisions. I was once asked to revise and resubmit a paper six times to the same outlet. Although frustrating, I channeled that frustration into working on that paper, and finally, it received an acceptance letter. Also, please do not be intimidated by a journal's rejection rate. That journal to which I submitted my papers six times had a rejection rate of about 75 percent. Well, by rejecting my paper six times and accepting it once, on the seventh submission, my paper actually increased that journal's rejection rate, and my paper still got published.

Concluding Thoughts

Earlier in this chapter, I advised treating the publication process as a game, much like the TV show *Survivor* is itself a game. Understandably, that's easier said than done; however, in the end, you will benefit from having some fun and a strategy as you would with any other game. I wish I could provide a fail-proof guide to getting your paper published, but any such guide would not be honest. There is no magical formula to getting your work successfully through the peer-review process. However, if you invest the time and energy in preparing to write, hold yourself accountable for writing, and perhaps most importantly, never give up on your paper no matter the hurdles tossed in your path, good things will eventually happen. Not always.

And certainly there is a steep learning curve in this game. But to paraphrase Yogi Berra, the harder I work, the luckier I get.

References

Allen, J., and S. Robbins. 2010. "Effects of Interest-Major Congruence, Motivation, and Academic Performance on Timely Degree Attainment." *Journal of Counseling Psychology* 57: 23–35.

Bem, D. J. 2004. "Writing the Empirical Journal Article." In *The Compleat Academic: A Career Guide,* edited by J. M. Darley, M. P. Zanna, and H. L. Roediger III, 2nd ed., 185–219. Washington, DC: American Psychological Association.

Casillas, A., S. Robbins, J. Allen, Y. L. Kuo, M. A. Hanson, and C. Schmeiser. 2012. "Predicting Early Academic Failure in High School from Prior Academic Achievement, Psychosocial Characteristics, and Behavior." *Journal of Educational Psychology* 104: 407–420.

Dunn, D. S., and S. B. Zaremba. 1997. "Thriving at Liberal Arts Colleges: The More Compleat Academic." *Teaching of Psychology* 24: 8–14.

Locke, E., and G. P. Latham. 1990. *A Theory of Goal Setting and Task Performance.* Englewood Cliffs, NJ: Prentice-Hall.

ANDREW N. CHRISTOPHER *is the chair of the Psychology Department at Albion College in Michigan.*

NEW DIRECTIONS FOR TEACHING AND LEARNING • DOI: 10.1002/tl

This chapter discusses ways that faculty development and teaching centers can foster the practice of SoTL and create a campus culture where SoTL is recognized as important scholarly work.

Faculty Development Centers and the Role of SoTL

Beth M. Schwartz, Aeron Haynie

In the recent past, higher education did not commonly address pedagogical practices of college faculty (Boyer 1990). Universities assumed that faculty members could effectively teach in their area of expertise and that knowledge of a subject matter would translate into good teaching. However, scholars of teaching and learning began to emphasize the need to identify best practices. When presenting best practices at national and international conferences focused on pedagogy, many administrators and instructors in higher education took notice (Hutchings, Huber, and Ciccone 2011). In response, during the last three decades, centers for teaching and learning appeared across the country. These centers, with names such as "center for teaching excellence," "teaching enhancement center," or "the center for teaching and learning," all focus on the same goal: train faculty to be more effective teachers, and in turn improve student learning. Through these centers faculty members:

- obtain peer-review assessments,
- learn how to align classroom goals with course assessments,
- partner with a mentor or more senior faculty member on campus for continued guidance on their teaching,
- obtain training on how to teach online and other nontraditional contexts, and
- discuss specific challenges they face in the classroom.

In addition to serving as catalysts for best practices in teaching, centers ideally promote a more scholarly approach to teaching, one that encourages faculty to use the methodology most appropriate for their disciplines to promote student learning. A campus teaching and learning center is a key tool in communicating and promoting the use of SoTL (Scholarship of Teaching

NEW DIRECTIONS FOR TEACHING AND LEARNING, no. 136, Winter 2013 © 2013 Wiley Periodicals, Inc.
Published online in Wiley Online Library (wileyonlinelibrary.com) • DOI: 10.1002/tl.20079

and Learning) across campus. In this chapter, we first explore ways to create a campus where SoTL is valued. Next we discuss issues to consider in structuring and staffing a teaching center to foster SoTL. Finally, we discuss specific programs to mentor and train faculty engaged in SoTL.

Creating a Campus Where SoTL Counts

Boyer (1990) broadened the definition of scholarship to include discovery, integration, application, and teaching. As a result, many campuses embrace a more inclusive definition that allows for a variety of different types of scholarship. In turn, diverse types of scholarship are considered worthy of recognition and valuable for faculty during reappointment, tenure, and promotion. SoTL is often categorized under the scholarship of teaching, where the purpose of the research is to examine pedagogical practices and achieve optimal learning. However, it could also be argued that, depending on the research program in question, SoTL could be easily categorized as scholarship of discovery (traditional research that builds new knowledge) or as scholarship of integration (interdisciplinary examination of knowledge). Regardless of the fit within different categories of scholarship, debate continues as to whether SoTL should be considered scholarship equal to more traditional avenues of research. In turn, there is still debate at many institutions as to how scholarship on teaching and learning, otherwise known as pedagogical research (Gurung and Schwartz 2009), fits within instructors' professional development. One of the important roles of a teaching center is to provide opportunities for faculty to learn more about the scholarship of teaching and learning through learning communities, public presentations by faculty engaged in SoTL work, and individual consultations.

The scholarship of teaching and learning has been gaining attention and respect for at least a decade. But with additional scrutiny came adjustments to the term used to define an emerging field. In earlier years, faculty began a research program on the *scholarship of teaching* in the same way that one would investigate what is considered a more traditional research program. Scholarship of teaching, coined by Boyer (1990), has since transformed to the *scholarship of teaching and learning*, a change in terminology that could be in part due to the increased attention on assessment at all colleges and universities. Accrediting agencies often request that administrators and faculty provide evidence of student learning set forth in each faculty member's classroom and the college's mission statement. What better way than to ask those teaching to assist with measuring student learning? However, a change in terminology could also be the result of faculty realizing that the ultimate measure of student success is improved student learning. The more inclusive term, *scholarship of teaching and learning*, is consistent with that notion (Hutchings, Huber, and Ciccone 2011). Rather than simply focus on a pedagogical change that took place, those in the field began to focus on what learning goal was achieved, with a description of the pedagogical change that allowed the change to occur. A shift toward learning led to many useful new assessment measures for determining the impact of change in teaching (Hutchings, Huber, and Ciccone 2011).

With the increase in SoTL, many instructors also began using the SoTL literature when making pedagogical choices in the classroom. As scholars in the field point out, conducting SoTL and using SoTL as a scholarly teacher should be made clearly distinctive in order for SoTL to be considered legitimate scholarship (Gurung and Schwartz 2009). Scholarly teaching can best be used to describe teaching that is informed by current research in teaching and learning. For example, an instructor may read what types of science lab techniques lead to the most gains in student learning, or an instructor may look at how different writing processes decrease the achievement gap between minority and nonminority students. Scholarly teaching can help inexperienced (and experienced!) college instructors teach based on the most recent published research. However, if an instructor reviews the literature and then gathers evidence from her own courses and shares her findings, she has moved beyond scholarly teaching to the scholarship of teaching and learning.

Although further progress is necessary, many administrators now recognize SoTL as valuable scholarly activity equal to that of disciplinary research. The increasing institutional requirement for student-learning assessment and the increase in more administrative support lead to more faculty engaged in pedagogical research. Vital to growth is a continued and expanded understanding of SoTL as true scholarship. Fortunately, a growing number of institutions recognize Boyer's model and are supportive of all forms of scholarship. When institutional support is paired with departmental support, more and more faculty members consider SoTL when choosing an area of research. Supportive departments are respectful of their colleagues' particular strengths, view all faculty members as equals, accept peer assessment and student evaluations as valuable sources for continued improvement, and provide equal incentives for teaching, scholarship, and service (Massy, Wilger, and Colbeck 2000).

As Hutchings, Huber, and Ciccone (2011) state, SoTL has come a long way since Boyer's original 1990 publication, and the culture of many colleges and universities is changing with regard to what is considered scholarship. However, not all institutions, departments, or colleagues are on board, making further progress necessary. Suggestions proposed to develop further support for SoTL include (1) a clear articulation on what constitutes SoTL work, (2) the presence of reward systems at both the departmental and institutional levels that recognize SoTL, and (3) training future academics with an appreciation of SoTL and how it equates to the more traditional approaches of scholarship (Gurung et al. 2008).

The ongoing challenge for any faculty member is to balance the responsibilities of the job that include teaching, research, and service. Of course, if SoTL is not deemed acceptable scholarship, most faculty members would not likely devote time out of their increasingly busy schedules to this type of scholarship. Rather, most would conduct research in the more traditional areas to fulfill the scholarship component evaluated for reappointment, tenure, and promotion. In fact, faculty members' disciplinary styles of inquiry may not easily translate to methodology used to conduct SoTL research, requiring a commitment to learn new techniques.

Often a director of a teaching and learning center can make significant strides within a campus culture to educate both faculty and administrators about SoTL. For example, a director can educate department chairs on how to develop the characteristics that create a supportive environment for all types of scholarship (Massy, Wilger, and Colbeck 2000). To reach the goal of support for all types of scholarship, those evaluating a faculty member must come to understand the value of pedagogical research; SoTL is equivalent in value to traditional scholarship. Some faculty members might already be *scholarly teachers*, approaching their classroom informed by the literature on teaching and learning, but they shun SoTL because the university fails to value such work. A more inclusive definition of scholarship can start with the faculty handbook, where the language used to define scholarship can explicitly include pedagogical research or SoTL. Administrative support of campus programming on scholarship could also include presentations focused on pedagogy to publicize further the institutions' commitment to all forms of research. If possible, job ads could indicate an interest in candidates with SoTL experience.

Faculty Development Centers: Staff, Structure, and Mission

The skills and training of the staff at a teaching and learning center need to be diverse to address the programming identified as most essential. Centers vary in size and make-up, but most comprise a faculty director, instructional designers, support staff, student workers, and a faculty advisory group of some kind. It is helpful if the director of a teaching center is a tenured faculty member who understands the mission of the institution. Further, the director should understand the concerns of faculty, have their regard, and be able to design programs that will appeal to faculty interests. Some centers utilize codirectors (e.g., someone familiar with quantitative research such as from the sciences or social sciences and a director more familiar with qualitative research from the humanities, education, or the arts). To be helpful to all faculty, directors should be open to diverse disciplinary methodologies.

When administrators identify the need for a teaching and learning center on campus, the staffing and programming decisions made must align with the institutional goals and mission. To connect the goals of the center to the goals and mission of the institution, it is important to identify what led to the recognition of a need for a center. Perhaps new faculty lack sufficient pedagogical training, there is a need for more effective assessment in the classroom, or faculty might be interested in conducting scholarship on teaching and learning (SoTL). Regardless of what identified needs led to the development of a center, typically, the first task of a new director is to conduct a *needs analysis* using focus groups, interviews, and surveys of members of the institution to identify campus needs. Needs identified through assessment will guide the type of programming and staffing developed at the center. Broad assessment across the campus will allow for the involvement of faculty in the development of programming, which in turn typically leads to an increase in faculty attending the programming offered (Gurung and Schwartz 2009). With a good fit between the needs of the institution and the center and with involvement of the faculty to determine the programming offered, faculty on campus likely will support the center's mission. Buy-in is essential for the success of any new center of teaching and learning.

In addition to an initial needs analysis, a center must commit to continual assessment to make sure the mission remains in focus. Otherwise, the center may be abolished or funding removed, which effectively cripples activity. In fact, like all programs on a campus, a center of teaching and learning must work to be viewed as viable and necessary. Economic constraints can put many center's resources in jeopardy. Financial decisions are often made based on an assessment of the success of the programming provided. To illustrate interest and attendance at programming, a director should keep records of the number of faculty and staff utilizing the center. In addition, a clear marketing strategy is essential to ensure that others on campus are aware of what the center offers. Holton (2002) provides a concise list of how to promote the programs offered, including using program reminders, involving public-relations staff on campus, publishing an article about programming in an internal publication, knowing the needs of faculty, and clearly communicating what faculty will learn from the programs offered. Most importantly, in today's climate, a coherent assessment plan indicating faculty professional growth is the best approach to maintaining financial resources (O'Meara, Terosky, and Neumann 2008).

Promoting the scholarship of teaching and learning—in particular, the use of evidence to demonstrate and evaluate student learning—dovetails with the increase in focus on assessment at all institutions of higher education, in particular from accrediting agencies across the country (see Gurung and Landrum 2012). That is, accrediting agencies want accountability. Institutions are called upon to provide evidence that students are achieving the goals set forth both at the institutional level (i.e., the mission) and at the classroom level. When faced with assessment requirements, many institutions find that providing evidence requires knowledge beyond most faculty members' expertise. As a result, colleges and universities developed centers where staff members with expertise in assessment and higher education could assist with assessment (Stefani 2011). In turn, faculty learned how to develop appropriate measures to assess student learning and how to make pedagogical choices that connect to student-learning outcomes. Indeed, to assess if any change in pedagogy is effective, the most obvious assessment would be student learning. A connection between teaching and learning provides the necessary avenue through which faculty can identify if changes are needed to improve student learning. Thus, although accrediting agencies focus on proof of effectiveness, the process of assessment fosters change within the classroom. Centers of teaching and learning have been pivotal to improve student learning through faculty training.

In addition to increasing the effectiveness of face-to-face teaching, centers support teachers in the use of instructional technology. With many technological advances in the last two decades, more and more faculty have incorporated technology in the classroom. Current technology includes the use of personal response systems (i.e., clickers), SmartBoards, tablets, MOOCS (Massively Open Online Courses), learning analytics, and the use of digital media (Johnson et al. 2013).

Particular technological challenges are faced when teaching online or hybrid courses (i.e., both face-to-face and online). Many institutions, partially in response to students' demands for greater schedule flexibility and partially because online education is a source of revenue for institutions, have begun to consider online course/program offerings (Mehrotra and McGahey 2012). Instructors face particular challenges when teaching online or hybrid courses. First, many faculty members are inexperienced in online teaching. Although familiar with the traditional classroom environment, faculty members may not be familiar with new technologies, and most have never taken an online course themselves. As a result, centers of teaching and learning have started to address the pedagogical challenges and differences instructors must be aware of when teaching online. Mehrotra and McGahey (2012) identified a number of factors distinct to an online course: the technical environment, instructional methods, assessment, and the learning experience of the students enrolled in the course. Interesting questions arise in the online environment such as how can an instructor best encourage class discussion or group-work online? What technologies can best help fight against plagiarism? Fortunately, many teaching centers now employ instructional designers who are trained to aid faculty to incorporate technology into teaching.

Although instructional technology is intriguing due to constant changes, it is imperative that teaching centers function as more than a place where faculty can learn specific (technical or instructional) skills. Technology has a way of getting attention, sometimes to the exclusion of other teaching issues. A center of teaching and learning must be careful to maintain a broad focus. Centers must be places where faculty discuss the larger implications of changing pedagogies and explore cutting-edge research on how students learn.

Disseminating SoTL

The definition of SoTL requires that findings be shared with others. Staff members in the Center for Teaching and Learning (CTL) are valuable resources when it comes to assisting faculty with the dissemination of findings. In addition to discipline-specific conferences that often include teaching-focused presentations, many teaching-focused venues are available. Avenues for SoTL dissemination include: (1) conferences held both nationally and internationally that are teaching-focused (e.g., International Society for the Scholarship of Teaching and Learning annual conference), (2) an increasing number of discipline-specific SoTL publications (e.g., *Teaching of Psychology, Pedagogy*), and (3) interdisciplinary SoTL-focused journals with articles included from all fields (e.g., *Journal of Higher Education*) (Gurung and Schwartz 2009). CTL staff or academic administrators could also arrange for SoTL presentations on campus, providing a more public avenue for colleagues to discuss their research with peers.

How to Use a Teaching Center for SoTL: Creating Faculty Communities of Practice

The most powerful way to convince faculty members of the importance of a scholarly teaching approach is to give them opportunities for inquiry. Faculty members can use their disciplinary methods to investigate student learning in their own courses. There are a number of ways that teaching centers can encourage SoTL work among faculty. CTL programming can include (1) individual consultations with faculty in a department that supports SoTL research, (2) funding SoTL start-up grants for faculty who have started SoTL research, (3) referrals to experienced SoTL researchers on campus, (4) publicizing SoTL publications and conferences, and (5) offering campus-wide Teaching Scholars programs. Facilitated by a member of the CTL staff, Teaching Scholars programs are usually yearlong and sometimes referred to as Faculty Learning Communities. Small groups of faculty from different disciplines meet on a regular basis to discuss the scholarship of teaching (Cox 2001). Projects can be individual or group research, and members of the team encourage and support each other as research occurs. Importantly, all conversations that occur within the community should be confidential, and the program should never be used for any evaluative purpose (see Tables 9.1 and 9.2). SoTL-focused groups function best at institutions where scholarly teaching already occurs. Teaching Scholars programs, in particular, have been quite successful on University of Wisconsin campuses; also, the University of Wisconsin–system offers a state-wide Teaching Scholars and Fellows Program that serves all branch colleges and universities. Several faculty who participated in the Teaching Scholars Program at the University of Wisconsin–Green Bay have gone on to publish significant

Table 9.1. Examples of Successful Teaching-Scholars Programs

Michigan State's The Center for the Scholarship of Teaching and Learning	http://fod.msu.edu/opportunities /lilly-teaching-fellows-program
Indiana University's Communities of Inquiry	http://citl.indiana.edu/programs/sotl /funded-sotl-projects.php
Maricopa Community College (MIL)	http://www.mcli.dist.maricopa.edu/mil
St Olaf College CILA Associates	http://wp.stolaf.edu/cila/associates/
Mount Royal University's Nexen Scholars Program	http://www.mtroyal.ca/ProgramsCourses /FacultiesSchoolsCentres/Institutefor ScholarshipofTeachingLearning/Signature Programs/index.htm
Vanderbilt University: SoTL Scholars program for graduate students	http://cft.vanderbilt.edu/programs /sotl-scholars-program/
Teaching Scholars and Fellows: 3 separate programs at Georgia Tech	http://www.cetl.gatech.edu/faculty/tfs
Stanford University Medical School Teaching Scholars	http://med.stanford.edu/anesthesia /education/teaching_scholars.html
Online program at West Virginia University	http://www.hsc.wvu.edu /Faculty-Development /Teaching-Scholars-Program
University of British Columbia Faculty SoTL Leadership Program	http://international.educ.ubc.ca/SOTL/

Table 9.2. Suggested Books/Articles for Campus Teaching Scholars Groups

Ambrose, S., M. Bridges, M. DiPietro, and M. Lovett. 2010. *How Learning Works: 7 Research-Based Principles for Smart Teaching.* San Francisco: Jossey-Bass.

Angelo, T. A., and K. Patricia Cross. 1994. *Classroom Assessment Techniques: A Handbook for College Teachers,* 2nd ed. San Francisco: Jossey-Bass.

Bain, K. 2004. *What the Best College Teachers Do.* Cambridge, MA: Harvard University Press.

Davis, B. G. 2003. *Tools for Teaching.* San Francisco: Jossey-Bass.

Fink, L. D. 2003. *Creating Significant Learning Experiences: An Integrated Approach to Designing College Courses.* San Francisco: Jossey-Bass.

Gurung, R. A. R, N. L. Chick, and A. Haynie. 2009. *Exploring Signature Pedagogies: Approaches to Teaching Disciplinary Habits of Mind.* Arlington, VA: Stylus.

Marton, F., D. Hounsell, and N. Entwistle. 1997. *The Experience of Learning: Implications for Teaching and Studying in Higher Education,* 2nd ed. Edinburgh: Scottish Academic Press.

Mazur, E. 1997. *Peer Instruction: A User's Manual.* Upper Saddle River, NJ: Prentice Hall.

Nelson, C. E. 2010. "Dysfunctional Illusions of Rigor: Lessons of Scholarship of Teaching and Learning." *To Improve the Academy* 28: 177–192.

SoTL research, serve as directors of the state-wide Teaching Scholars Program, and become leaders in their discipline's SoTL work.

At universities without a strong tradition of SoTL, a cautious approach might include offering learning communities that introduce faculty to "scholarly teaching," where members of the community read published teaching research. Next, faculty members can begin to ask their own questions. (Middendorf's [2004] work with Freshman Learning Communities that examines learning "bottlenecks" and her "Decoding the Disciplines" model are excellent starting points for faculty who want to identify areas in need of research.) As a final goal in learning communities, original scholarship (SoTL) can occur, with the teaching community supporting the process. If faculty are rushed through the process of embracing the scholarship of teaching and learning, poor-quality projects might further faculty perception that SoTL is not legitimate scholarship. In addition, faculty unfamiliar with SoTL but interested in learning more about teaching and learning may be discouraged from attempting to complete a SoTL project.

In order for Teaching Scholars programs to succeed, participation in the program must be both competitive and compensated. Participants should be chosen based on evidence of teaching excellence, which will make successful completion more likely. In the first few years of a new program, it is wise to recruit participants from across disciplines in order to increase visibility of the program and create a more diverse community. It is also useful to explain to department chairs and deans the value of such programs. Compensation varies by campus, ranging from a $1,000 honorarium to two course releases for one academic year. The level of compensation tells faculty how much the administration values the program and also signals how much time faculty members should devote to the project. Of course, an additional incentive is the opportunity to develop a publishable study. A publication relies on the final step of conducting SoTL rather than merely discussing teaching articles.

The benefits of a successful Teaching Scholars program go beyond just the publications generated; cross disciplinary discussions of teaching help demonstrate the common challenges we all face and require us to articulate our teaching goals to faculty outside of our disciplines. As Middendorf (2004) describes the FLC at Indiana University, when a faculty member does not understand a colleague's lesson plan, it is difficult to blame the student for lack of effort. Explaining a discipline's core values to a thoughtful colleague can be the first step in exploring individual pedagogy (Gurung, Chick, and Haynie 2008).

Although broad discussions of teaching and learning should not be undervalued, the current climate of higher education necessitates that Teaching Scholars programs deliver tangible results in some fashion. In addition to traditional publication, dissemination might come in the form of public presentations of scholars' findings and summaries on teaching center web sites. For example, many programs invite the previous year's scholars to present the results of their studies at the first meeting of the new scholars. Publicizing the work of teaching scholars both encourages future applicants and strengthens continued support for funding. Letters recognizing a faculty member's work should also be sent out to each participant's department chair and publicized in appropriate venues.

NEW DIRECTIONS FOR TEACHING AND LEARNING • DOI: 10.1002/tl

Deciding which methods for promoting SoTL will work best depends on many factors: the campus identity (whether a research-intensive or teaching-focused), support from administration, level of SoTL experience among faculty, relationship of faculty to the teaching center, and general campus culture. Just as good teaching often begins by collecting information on students, successful campus SoTL programs are tailored to the particular faculty community they serve. For example, faculty members with heavy teaching loads might be responsive to programs that help them leverage their extensive teaching experience into research. (Of course, this strategy only works when SoTL publications count toward tenure and promotion.) Research-intensive institutions are traditionally less likely to value and reward SoTL, since these projects generally fall outside narrowly defined definitions of faculty disciplinary expertise. Faculty not trained in qualitative analysis, for example, may need reassurance that they do not have to become social scientists in order to conduct SoTL. Faculty members also should be given strong examples of SoTL work as well as help with navigating the Institutional Review Board (IRB) process. For example, the University of Michigan's CRTL offers "Investigating student learning" grants and handles much of the IRB process for faculty, thereby encouraging participation in SoTL (Cook et al. 2001).

Conclusion

In conclusion, college and university teaching centers are leading the SoTL movement, both by providing SoTL-based "Teaching Scholars" programs and through encouraging a larger number of faculty to base their pedagogical decisions on empirically based SoTL literature. Although not all faculty members are willing or able to conduct their own SoTL research, all faculty should be made aware of the vast resources available for making decisions about teaching and learning. Centers for teaching and learning therefore provide the knowledge base for those who strive to be scholarly teachers and those who choose to be scholars of teaching and learning. With the right fit between the institution's mission and the center's programming as well as a knowledgeable director who involves faculty and staff when determining what is offered, all constituents will benefit from a teaching and learning center.

References

Boyer, E. L. 1990. *Scholarship Reconsidered: Priorities of the Professoriate*. San Francisco: Jossey-Bass.

Cook, C. E., M. Kaplan, J. Nidiffer, and M. Wright. 2001, November. "Preparing Future Faculty–Faster." *AAHE Bulletin* 34 (3): 3–7.

Cox, M. D. 2001. "Faculty Learning Communities: Change Agents for Transforming Institutions into Learning Organizations." *To Improve the Academy* 19: 69–93.

New Directions for Teaching and Learning • DOI: 10.1002/tl

Gurung, R. A. R., P. I. Ansburg, P. A. Alexander, N. K. Lawrence, and D. E. Johnson. 2008. "The State of the Scholarship of Teaching and Learning in Psychology." *Teaching of Psychology* 35: 249–261.

Gurung, R. A. R, N. L. Chick, and A. Haynie. 2008. *Exploring Signature Pedagogies: Approaches to Teaching Disciplinary Habits of Mind*. Arlington, VA: Stylus.

Gurung, R. A. R., and R. E. Landrum. 2012. "Assessment and the Scholarship of Teaching and Learning." In *Assessing Teaching and Learning in Psychology: Current and Future Perspectives*, edited by D. Dunn, S. C. Baker, C. M. Mehrotra, R. E. Landrum, and M. McCarthy, 159–171. Belmont, CA: Cengage.

Gurung, R. A. R., and B. M. Schwartz. 2009. *Optimizing Teaching and Learning: Practicing Pedagogical Research*. West Sussex, UK: Wiley-Blackwell.

Holton, S. A. 2002. "Promoting Your Professional Development Program." In *A Guide to Faculty Development: Practical Advice, Examples, and Resources*, edited by K. H. Gillespie, 100–107. Bolton, MA: Anker Publishing.

Hutchings, P., M. T. Huber, and A. Ciccone. 2011. "Getting There: An Integrative Vision of the Scholarship of Teaching and Learning." *International Journal for the Scholarship of Teaching and Learning* 5: 1–14. http://digitalcommons.georgiasouthern.edu/int_jtl/223/.

Johnson, L., S. Adams-Becker, M. Cummins, V. Estrada, A. Freeman, and H. Ludgate. 2013. *NMC Horizon Report: 2013 Higher Education Edition*. Austin, TX: The New Media Consortium.

Massy, W., A. Wilger, and C. Colbeck. 2000. "Overcoming 'Hallowed' Colleagiality: Department Cultures and Teaching Quality." In *Learning from Change: Landmarks in Teaching and Learning from Change Magazine 1969–1999*, edited by D. DeSure, 28–32. Sterling, VA: Stylus Publishing.

Mehrotra, C. M., and L. McGahey. 2012. "Online Teaching." In *Evidence-Based Teaching for Higher Education*, edited by B. M. Schwartz and R. A. R. Gurung, 59–76. Washington, DC: American Psychological Association.

Middendorf, J. 2004. "Facilitating a Faculty Learning Community Using the Decoding the Disciplines Model." In *Decoding the Disciplines: Helping Students Learn Disciplinary Ways of Thinking*, New Directions for Teaching and Learning, no. 98, edited by D. Pace and J. Middendorf, 95–107. San Francisco: Jossey-Bass.

O'Meara, K., A. L. Terosky, and A. Neumann. 2008. "Faculty Careers and Work Lives: A Professional Growth Perspective." Special issue, *ASHE Higher Education Report* 34 (3).

Stefani, L. 2011. *Evaluating the Effectiveness of Academic Development: Principles and Practice*. New York: Routledge.

BETH M. SCHWARTZ *is a professor of psychology and the assistant dean of Randolph College.*

AERON HAYNIE *is the director of the Center for Teaching Excellence and an associate professor of English, University of New Mexico.*

NEW DIRECTIONS FOR TEACHING AND LEARNING • DOI: 10.1002/tl

INDEX

Academic assessment, coordinated, 15
Academic program assessment cycle, 11
Adams, C. M., 19
Addison, W., 3
Adelman, C., 75
Alexander, P. A., 103
Allen, J., 92
Altman, C., 3
American Psychological Association (APA) style, 57, 76–78, 80–82
Analysis of covariance (ANCOVA), 56
ANCOVA. *See* Analysis of covariance (ANCOVA)
Angelo, T. A., 10
Ansburg, P. I., 103
Anthis, K., 24, 25
Appleton, J. J., 19
Armistead, L., 56
Assessment, 18–19; coordinated with SoTL, 12–15; to enhance student learning, 10–11; to identify bottlenecks in learning, 14

Baker, S. C., 1, 38
Barak, M., 27
Baron, R. M., 44, 45
Bartsch, R. A., 4, 17, 20, 28, 30, 33, 35, 37, 38, 41, 42, 48
Bass, R., 9
Bates, K. A., 41
Beech, J. R., 82
Beers, M. J., 73
Beins, A. M., 82
Beins, B. C., 82
Belmont Report, The, 61, 68, 70
Bem, D. J., 82, 89
Benassi, V. A., 1
Berkman, E. T., 56
Bernstein, D., 3
Between-groups design, 55–56
Between-participants designs, 26–28
Bishop-Clark, C., 2
Bittner, W. M. E., 30, 41, 42
Bjork, R. A., 20
Borden, L. M., 28
Borg, W. R., 22, 29, 36, 38

Boyer, E. L., 2, 101, 102, 103
Braver, S. L., 26
Bridges, G. S., 41
Burnett, A. N., 2, 3
Buskist, W., 1, 52

Campbell, D. T., 18, 19, 22, 24–26, 28–30, 36–43
Carnegie Foundation for the Advancement of Teaching, 1
Case, K. A., 37
Casillas, A., 92
Causal studies, hypotheses for, 18–19
Center for Teaching and Learning (CTL), 107
Chang, K. E., 40
Chen, S. F., 40
Chesbro, J. L., 44
Chick, N. L., 13, 109
Christenson, S. L., 19
Christopher, A. N., 4, 85, 99
Ciccone, A., 1, 3, 7, 8, 101–103
Classroom studies, designs for, 38–46; crossover design, 42–43; interrupted time-series design, 43–44; mediators and, 45; moderators and, 44–45; multiple treatments, 44; one-group post-test only design, 39; one-group pre-test/post-test design, 40–41; simple correlation, 38–39; two-group post-test only design, 39–40; two-group pre-test/post-test design, 41–42; within-participants design, 42
Cobern, K., 20, 28, 42
Cohen, J., 53, 54
Colbeck, C., 103, 104
Cole, M. S., 44
Collins, D., 28
Conditions, construct validity, 23–26; different sections, 25; control condition, 24–25; participant expectancies, 25; researcher expectancies, 25–26; treatment condition, 24
Conditions, internal validity, 26–30; counterbalancing, 29; covariates, 27–28; random assignment, 26–27
Confounds, 24

113

NEW DIRECTIONS FOR TEACHING AND LEARNING
ORDER FORM SUBSCRIPTION AND SINGLE ISSUES

DISCOUNTED BACK ISSUES:

Use this form to receive 20% off all back issues of *New Directions for Teaching and Learning*.
All single issues priced at **$23.20** (normally $29.00)

TITLE	ISSUE NO.	ISBN
_____	_____	_____
_____	_____	_____
_____	_____	_____

Call 888-378-2537 or see mailing instructions below. When calling, mention the promotional code JBNND to receive your discount. For a complete list of issues, please visit www.josseybass.com/go/ndtl

SUBSCRIPTIONS: (1 YEAR, 4 ISSUES)

☐ New Order   ☐ Renewal

U.S.	☐ Individual: $89	☐ Institutional: $311
CANADA/MEXICO	☐ Individual: $89	☐ Institutional: $351
ALL OTHERS	☐ Individual: $113	☐ Institutional: $385

Call 888-378-2537 or see mailing and pricing instructions below.
Online subscriptions are available at www.onlinelibrary.wiley.com

ORDER TOTALS:

Issue / Subscription Amount: $ _____

Shipping Amount: $ _____
(for single issues only – subscription prices include shipping)

Total Amount: $ _____

SHIPPING CHARGES:
First Item $6.00
Each Add'l Item $2.00

(No sales tax for U.S. subscriptions. Canadian residents, add GST for subscription orders. Individual rate subscriptions must be paid by personal check or credit card. Individual rate subscriptions may not be resold as library copies.)

BILLING & SHIPPING INFORMATION:

☐ **PAYMENT ENCLOSED:** *(U.S. check or money order only. All payments must be in U.S. dollars.)*

☐ **CREDIT CARD:** ☐ VISA ☐ MC ☐ AMEX

Card number _____Exp. Date_____

Card Holder Name_____Card Issue #_____

Signature _____Day Phone_____

☐ **BILL ME:** *(U.S. institutional orders only. Purchase order required.)*

Purchase order #_____
    Federal Tax ID 13559302 • GST 89102-8052

Name_____

Address_____

Phone_____ E-mail_____

Copy or detach page and send to: **John Wiley & Sons, One Montgomery Street, Suite 1200, San Francisco, CA 94104-4594**

Order Form can also be faxed to: **888-481-2665**

PROMO JBNND

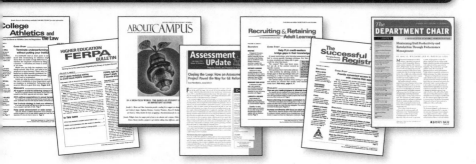

Statement of Ownership

Statement of Ownership, Management, and Circulation (required by 39 U.S.C. 3685), filed on OCTOBER 1, 2013 for NEW DIRECTIONS FOR TEACHING AND LEARNING (Publication No. 0271-0633), published Quarterly for an annual subscription price of $89 at Wiley Subscription Services, Inc., at Jossey-Bass, One Montgomery St., Suite 1200, San Francisco, CA 94104-4594.

The names and complete mailing addresses of the Publisher, Editor, and Managing Editor are: Publisher, Wiley Subscription Services, Inc., A Wiley Company at San Francisco, One Montgomery St., Suite 1200, San Francisco, CA 94104-4594; Editor, Catherine M. Wehlburg, TCU Box 297028, Texas Christian University, Fort Worth TX 76129; Managing Editor, None. Contact Person: Joe Schuman; Telephone: 415-782-3232.

NEW DIRECTIONS FOR TEACHING AND LEARNING is a publication owned by Wiley Subscription Services, Inc., 111 River St., Hoboken, NJ 07030. The known bondholders, mortgages, and other security holders owning or holding 1% or more of total amount of bonds, mortgages, or other securities are (see list).

	Average No. Copies Each Issue During Preceding 12 Months	No. Copies of Single Issue Published Nearest To Filing Date (Summer 2013)
15a. Total number of copies (net press run)	835	727
15b. Legitimate paid and/or requested distribution (by mail and outside mail)		
15b(1). Individual paid/requested mail subscriptions stated on PS form 3541 (include direct written request from recipient, telemarketing, and Internet requests from recipient, paid subscriptions including nominal rate subscriptions, advertiser's proof copies, and exchange copies)	302	282
15b(2). Copies requested by employers for distribution to employees by name or position, stated on PS form 3541	0	0
15b(3). Sales through dealers and carriers, street vendors, counter sales, and other paid or requested distribution outside USPS	0	0
15b(4). Requested copies distributed by other mail classes through USPS	0	0
15c. Total paid and/or requested circulation (sum of 15b(1), (2), (3), and (4))	302	282
15d. Nonrequested distribution (by mail and outside mail)		
15d(1). Outside county nonrequested copies stated on PS form 3541	7	6
15d(2). In-county nonrequested copies stated on PS form 3541	0	0
15d(3). Nonrequested copies distributed through the USPS by other classes of mail	0	0
15d(4). Nonrequested copies distributed outside the mail	0	0
15e. Total nonrequested distribution (sum of 15d(1), (2), (3), and (4))	7	6
15f. Total distribution (sum of 15c and 15e)	309	288
15g. Copies not distributed	526	439
15h. Total (sum of 15f and 15g)	835	727
15i. Percent paid and/or requested circulation (15c divided by 15f times 100)	98%	98%

I certify that all information furnished on this form is true and complete. I understand that anyone who furnishes false or misleading information on this form or who omits material or information requested on this form may be subject to criminal sanctions (including fines and imprisonment) and/or civil sanctions (including civil penalties).

Statement of Ownership will be printed in the Winter 2013 issue of this publication.

(signed) Susan E. Lewis, VP & Publisher-Periodicals